T0288011

THE FOUNDATION OF THE CIA

THE FOUNDATION
OF THE CIA

HARRY TRUMAN, THE MISSOURI
GANG, AND THE ORIGINS OF THE
COLD WAR

Richard E. Schroeder

UNIVERSITY OF MISSOURI PRESS
Columbia

Copyright © 2017 by
The Curators of the University of Missouri
University of Missouri Press, Columbia, Missouri 65211
Printed and bound in the United States of America
All rights reserved. First printing, 2017

ISBN: 978-0-8262-2137-7
Library of Congress Control Number: 2017941373

∞™ This paper meets the requirements of the
American National Standard for Permanence of Paper
for Printed Library Materials, Z39.48, 1984.

Typefaces: Masheen and Garamond

This book is dedicated to my mother, Rebecca Boies Schroeder, General Editor of the University of Missouri Press Missouri Heritage Reader Series, with thanks for her encouragement, love, and support. It is also dedicated to my wife, Leah Webb Schroeder, always equally encouraging, loving, and supportive. My particular thanks go to my fellow United States Government employees, especially those at the National Archives in Washington, DC, and Independence, Missouri, and to my fellow historians and professional colleagues at the Central Intelligence Agency for their advice and careful attention to my scholarship.

I am grateful that they have caught some of my errors, and am of course fully responsible for any errors that they missed.

Contents

Foreword

Almost from harry truman's first day in public life, people underestimated him, belittling or criticizing his background while ignoring the daunting challenges he faced. His opponents considered him at best a Midwest small-time farmer and failed shopkeeper, and at worst a corrupt politician in the pocket of big-city bosses. His friends and advisers faced similar scorn, again with little regard for the world they faced or the challenges and dangers before them.

On reflection, however, it is now clear that the end of World War II and Truman's presidency established the framework for the next forty years of American global leadership and the great competition between the West and international communism. Truman shared the global stage with such oversize personalities as Winston Churchill and Joseph Stalin, and inherited brilliant advisers, such as Fleet Admiral William Leahy and General of the Army George Marshall—both of whom served him faithfully throughout his presidency.

The great men known to history naturally played major roles in shaping the postwar world and the institutions of national security, but lesser-known figures, a surprising number from Missouri, also were at the center of Truman's drive to understand and influence this new and threatening world. A young Missouri lawyer named Clark Clifford came to the White House just as Truman was first meeting Churchill and Stalin in the ruins of Berlin, and a wealthy and successful Missouri businessman, Sidney Souers, joined Clifford and Leahy in drawing up the outline for a reorganized Defense Department and an American intelligence organization unique to world history. Souers became the first Director of Central Intelligence, responsible for giving Truman what no world leader before him had enjoyed: a "newspaper" compiling and analyzing the great international issues and threats facing the United States, and drawing upon the best intelligence collection and the most astute interpretation possible. Souers then became Truman's closest national security adviser and lifelong friend. Less than two years later, another Missourian, Rear Admiral Roscoe Hillenkoetter, became not only Director of Central Intelligence but first chief of the new American Central Intelligence Agency.

Regrettably, neither Souers nor Hillenkoetter has been recognized for their important roles in American intelligence supporting Harry Truman's foreign policy during those dangerous early years of the Cold War. As the third Director of Central Intelligence from Harry Truman's home state of Missouri, and as one who served in the U.S. Navy alongside Admirals Souers and Hillenkoetter in World War II, I welcome this reminder of the contributions made to American national security and intelligence by my fellow Missourians.

Judge William H. Webster,
Director, Federal Bureau of Investigation,
Director of Central Intelligence

Washington, DC
October 2016

THE FOUNDATION
OF THE CIA

Introduction

Harry s. truman became president in the final months of one great global war and was to lead the United States for the early years of a much longer global conflict. In many ways he took advantage of a strong team of wartime leaders, such as his military chief of staff, Fleet Admiral William D. Leahy, and wartime developments like the atomic bomb, but in other ways he broke dramatically from wartime institutions and policies. At the end of World War II, one of his most striking decisions was to dismiss the legendary Major General William "Wild Bill" Donovan and disband the Office of Strategic Services (OSS), America's first national intelligence agency. To many Americans, secret intelligence organizations raised fears of Nazi Germany's *Gestapo* (secret state police) or Communist Russia's KGB (Committee of State Security). The new president said that he did not want the United States to have such an agency in peacetime.

Truman, who became president with almost no knowledge of the American national security structure or foreign affairs, soon recognized that the end of world war did not mean the beginning of world peace. He also recognized that beyond weapons, soldiers, and generals, the United States needed spies, researchers and analysts, and an experienced intelligence manager to coordinate and lead American intelligence efforts and advise the president on critical national security questions, potential enemies, and external threats to the United States. As a lifelong student of history, Truman, better than many of his contemporaries, appreciated the challenges faced by his predecessors all the way back to George Washington and the mistakes the country had often made in its national security and international affairs policies. As he later claimed, "I got a couple of admirals together and they formed" the Central Intelligence Agency (CIA).[1] One of those admirals was his own military chief of staff and the first American five-star flag officer, Iowa native Fleet Admiral Leahy. Another was a member of what Truman's political enemies dubbed "the Missouri Gang" to suggest corrupt cronyism: Missouri businessman and wartime naval intelligence officer Rear Admiral Sidney W. Souers.[2] He took responsibility for the fledgling Central Intelligence Group after Truman had dismissed Donovan and abolished the OSS, and to the end of the Truman presidency, Souers continued as executive secretary and later "special consultant" to his new National Security Council (NSC).

A third admiral, Saint Louis native Roscoe Hillenkoetter, became the first statutory director of the new CIA, as well as the president's principal intelligence adviser. Even more than Souers, Hillenkoetter had extensive practical intelligence experience, as well as distinguished service as a sailor. After graduating with honors from the United States Naval Academy just after World War I, Hillenkoetter served in submarines, destroyers, and battleships. Interspersed with his sea duty was service as naval attaché to Paris, Madrid, and Lisbon in the 1930s and early 1940s. As a uniformed diplomatic "spy," he observed the victory of General Francisco Franco's Fascists with the help of the new Nazi German war machine in the Spanish Civil War. Shortly thereafter, he watched the defeat of France at the hands of the Germans in the spring of 1940. While in France, he earned the respect and admiration of Admiral Leahy, then ambassador to Vichy France and later senior military advisor to presidents Franklin Roosevelt and Harry Truman. Like fellow Missourian Commander Samuel Fuqua, who won the Medal of Honor as the senior surviving officer on *Arizona*, Hillenkoetter was the senior survivor on *West Virginia* during the surprise Japanese attack on the battlefleet at Pearl Harbor on December 7, 1941.

After experiencing firsthand at Pearl Harbor the deadly cost of America's failure to create a real national intelligence service, Hillenkoetter became senior intelligence officer for the Pacific Fleet before returning to sea duty in the Pacific naval war. After World War II, Leahy remembered Hillenkoetter's skills as an intelligence officer in Europe and recommended him as the first director of the new CIA. Together, Truman, Leahy, and the Missouri Gang of Souers, Hillenkoetter, and young White House lawyer Clark Clifford created the framework for what became the largest and most powerful intelligence structure in the world, doing so against fierce resistance from entrenched interests in the American military and U.S. Department of State. At the same time, they confronted staggering threats abroad from a suspicious, aggressive, and expansionist Soviet Union led by a paranoid dictator equipped with the world's largest army and legions of highly skilled spies. As the Soviets and their Asian allies seized control of the newly liberated countries of Eastern Europe and such Asian countries as China and North Korea, and Soviet spies stole the secret of the atomic bomb, the CIA quickly became engaged in leading the West's secret war against international communism, which did not end until forty years later, with the fall of the Berlin Wall and the collapse of the Soviet Union and its empire. This is the story of the first few years of that long struggle.

CHAPTER ONE

American National Intelligence
From the Revolutionary Army to World War II

DURING EARLY CRISES IN THE history of the United States, especially the American Revolution and the Civil War, national leaders recognized the need to find ways to better understand—and thus more easily defeat—enemies. Both the work of understanding foreign adversaries and the secret organizations that do so are called "intelligence." Many modern professionals consider General George Washington to have been the country's first director of national intelligence because he took such a personal interest in recruiting and managing spies to better understand his British opponents. Early American leaders like Benjamin Franklin and Thomas Jefferson quickly learned the skills of intelligence collection, analysis, and influence when they were dispatched abroad to European capitals, first and foremost as diplomats but equally important as collectors of useful secret information and advocates trying to persuade powerful Europeans to support the struggling American rebellion.

But if wartime leaders understood the need to understand their enemies, American leaders and generals in the first century of the republic quickly forgot those lessons as soon as the conflict had ended. European Great Powers had, however, been rivals for centuries, and in countries like England, France, and Russia, the skills of spying on other countries were almost as well developed as skills in creating new weapons and managing great armies and fleets. As an example, by the end of the American Civil War, the Union army was as well led and skillful as any fighting force in the world, and the American navy had a fleet as modern as any European rival. European observers watched these American advances with great interest, and they applied American lessons to their own countries. Within twenty years, however, as the United States focused its energy on absorbing millions of immigrants and developing the vast stretches of the American West, the navy shrank to such a state that even Brazil had a more powerful and advanced fleet, and in 1889 the American navy ranked as the twelfth largest in the world. Still, American naval officers observed foreign technological developments and naval conflicts with great attention, and they sent their reports back to Washington. Problems quickly arose, however, because each American observer had different opinions of foreign developments, and they sent those opinions to different offices within American naval headquarters. These offices, in turn, had different views about how the navy should spend its money and focus its meager resources, and Congress took unhappy note of this confusion. The last decades of the nineteenth century were a time of revolutionary technological advancement, and these advances were leading Europeans to build great battleships of such massive size, strength, and firepower that they were the superweapons of the period. The United States might have been a country with a flourishing international maritime trade, but without a real navy to defend the country against foreign fleets—or a clear picture of possible foreign threats—American ships or even coastal cities were vulnerable to destruction.

Therefore, in early 1882 the secretary of the navy directed the creation of an Office of Intelligence,[1] to be combined with the departmental library to collect and record information that would be useful to the navy in time of war or peace. All naval officers were directed to use "all opportunities . . . to collect and forward" what today would be called foreign naval intelligence.[2] Aside from officers on ships visiting foreign ports, the navy even sent officers to American embassies overseas to report on naval matters. The secretary directed that "only such officers as have shown an aptitude for intelligence staff work, or who by their intelligence and knowledge of foreign languages . . . give promise of such aptitude, should be employed." Reports from overseas all came back to this new Office of Naval Intelligence (ONI),[3] where overworked "clerks" could then analyze them, advise the secretary and Congress, and even publish a monthly bulletin to inform naval officers about the latest foreign developments. Today, the officers in the field would be called "collectors," and the clerks "analysts," but it took many decades, and many failures, to develop the very different skills needed by these two very different but equally important professions. And it took just as long to create the government organizations that would provide secret foreign intelligence to government leaders and Congress, and for those "customers" to understand and support these secret organizations.

The United States was delighted by the navy's success in the Spanish-American War of 1898, which left America occupying Cuba and the Philippines, but many Americans were alarmed by Japan's success in defeating Russia's fleet just seven years later in 1905. Anti-Asian feeling ran very high in California, especially after the great San Francisco earthquake in April 1906, and anti-Japanese laws and riots offended and angered Japan. War hysteria arose in popular newspapers in both countries, with the Japanese asking, "Why do we not insist on sending ships" to protect Japanese Americans from "the rascals of the United States, cruel and merciless like devils." President Theodore Roosevelt, a former assistant secretary of the navy, wanted a larger US fleet, but he raged at "the infernal fools in California" who

> insult the Japanese recklessly and the worse than criminal stupidity of the San Francisco mob, the . . . press, and . . . the *New York Herald*. I do not believe we will have war, but it is no fault of the . . . [tabloid] press if we do not have it. The Japanese seem to have about the same proportion of . . . prize [supernationalist] fools that we have.[4]

Californians became so frightened by the idea of Japanese naval attacks on their cities, in fact, that in 1907 Roosevelt used their appeals for help as an excuse to send his new American battle fleet around Cape Horn to the West Coast as part of his audacious plan to send the "Great White Fleet" around the world to demonstrate American strength and technology. Naval intelligence officers accompanied the fleet, taking careful note of all the South American and Asian navies that welcomed their visit, although one young intelligence officer wrote his mother, "Please don't tell anyone that officers . . . do such things because some people might think it wasn't . . . courteous."[5]

Just a few years later, in 1914, the Great War broke out in Europe, finding the United States not only unprepared but unwilling to become involved.[6] By now the Great White Fleet was shockingly obsolete, especially compared to the British and German battle fleets, and in any case Americans themselves were undecided about where their sympathies lay. The large number of German immigrants, especially in the Midwest, were naturally drawn to support their fatherland, and most Irish Americans were hostile to Great Britain because of British policy in Ireland. Because the products of American farms and factories were vital to the warring camps, both Germany and England tried very hard to influence the United States. German agents were especially aggressive in trying to recruit spies and saboteurs,[7] while the British tried to charm the American government while easily breaking and reading coded American diplomatic messages.[8] Thanks to the efforts of the new Bureau of Investigation (later named the Federal Bureau of Investigation [FBI]) and the United States Secret Service, President Woodrow Wilson gradually became aware of efforts by German diplomats to secretly influence American newspapers, subsidize Irish American and German American organizations, and plant bombs in ships bound for Great Britain. Both German army and naval attachés were involved, especially the very active German naval reserve officer Franz von Rintelen, who boasted, "I'll buy what I can and blow up what I can't."[9] In 1915 Wilson wrote: "I am sure that the country is honeycombed with German intrigue and infested with German spies. The evidence of these things are multiplying every day." He even worried "that there might be an armed uprising of German sympathizers. Rumors of preparations for such a thing have frequently reached us."

Although trying hard to remain neutral, Wilson couldn't ignore the evidence of German attempts to subvert Americans, especially since the British, who had captured von Rintelen on his way back to Germany, were adding alarming details to the information gathered by the Bureau of Investigation and the Secret Service. At the end of 1915, therefore, the United States expelled the German army and naval attachés. The secretary of state, Robert Lansing, complained of "attacks upon . . . American industries and commerce through incendiary fires and explosions in factories, threats to intimidate employers and other acts of violence." As he told President Wilson, "I feel we cannot wait any longer to act. . . . We have been overpatient with these people."[10]

The most shocking events turning not only the American people but also the government against Germany were the sinking by a German submarine of the British ocean liner *Lusitania* in 1915—with the loss of more than one hundred Americans—and the explosion of two million pounds of munitions meant for Russia on Black Tom Island in New York Harbor in 1916. German sabotage showed how vulnerable the United States was, but also that the American police and security services were all but incompetent. Not only were the Secret Service and Bureau of Investigation understaffed, underfunded, and undertrained, but they feuded with each other so much that they would not share information. For his part, Secretary Lansing proposed to create an information center in his department, telling President Wilson that the agencies were "willing to report to the State Department but not each other." This was not the first or last time that rivalries between government organizations would weaken American intelligence efforts. This was also not the last time that more sophisticated foreign intelligence officers benefited from American inexperience. In fact, the British intelligence chief in New York, Sir William Wiseman, soon won Wilson's confidence so powerfully that later a senior British officer called Wiseman "the most successful 'agent of influence' the British ever had."[11]

Because much German sabotage was directed against American shipping or port facilities, in 1916 the assistant secretary of the navy, Franklin Roosevelt, gained approval to create a group of naval investigators to be stationed in each domestic naval district to guard against enemy activity, detect foreign spies, and

Naval Attaché John A. Gade, who served in Europe in World Wars I and II (Naval History and Heritage Command, NH 49479).

protect American property and interests.[12] Initially, these counterintelligence officers were volunteer reservists rather than professional naval officers, and in 1929, more than a decade later, Missouri businessman Sidney Souers—later Harry Truman's first director of central intelligence—joined their ranks.

When the United States entered World War I on April 6, 1917, there were only a handful of US naval attachés stationed abroad, and those in Germany and Austria were expelled. Other offices in Europe were quickly opened, however, and the Office of Naval Intelligence needed candidates with foreign-language skills and experience. As Lieutenant Colonel James Breckinridge, the first US Marine naval attaché in Scandinavia, later said:

> We need two things, and we need them badly. These are a knowledge of languages away and beyond the usual American ability to stutter. . . . We are a joke in any international gathering. . . . The other thing is to have a small class in which to teach what intelligence duty is. . . . To begin with, [attachés] should know the language fluently, know the history of the people and the country, something about their social conditions and persuasions, their national ambitions and prejudices . . . . They then will be at home. . . . If [the attaché] is prepared for that sort of work, there is no limit to what he can do.[13]

One of the best-qualified of those new candidates was John Allyne Gade, the son of an American mother and Norwegian diplomat father. He grew up in Norway, was educated in France and Germany, studied architecture at Harvard University, and practiced successfully in New York until World War I inspired him to join an American aid organization in German-occupied Belgium. Aside from his humanitarian work, he engaged in anti-German intelligence "mischief" with Belgian secret agents. Once the United States entered the war, Gade was given a navy commission and made assistant naval attaché in Oslo, responsible for Norway and Sweden. Soon he was promoted to naval attaché in Denmark, and he made good use of his native Norwegian to recruit sailors who had access to very important information about German naval activities in the Baltic and North Seas. It was also extremely helpful that the admiral commanding the Danish coast guard was an old family friend. Gade worked closely with allied attachés but "found it humiliating to realize what a greenhorn I was in comparison with my [British and French] colleagues."[14]

Although the United States might have been new to the ruthless world of wartime espionage, Gade learned quickly. Ordered to steal the codes from the German embassy in Copenhagen, Gade learned that the senior German diplomat had a weakness for pretty women. He suggested finding a woman to seduce the German but was rebuked by the secretary of the navy himself for suggesting something so immoral. The navy, indeed the United States in general, had very ambivalent feelings about secret activities, from the young Great White Fleet intelligence officer who worried that collecting information about foreign navies was discourteous, to the secretary of the navy, the secretary of state, and the president—all of whom considered intelligence ungentlemanly. Undeterred, Gade learned from a naval intelligence colleague in New York about a young German American nurse who would agree to help Gade steal the codes. She was successful, and the codes were passed to Herbert Yardley, the father of modern American code-breaking and the US Army's chief cryptologist. A few weeks later the German diplomat caught the nurse copying more German codes, but Gade and a Danish naval officer were able to smuggle her out of the German embassy and then across the Baltic Sea to Sweden.[15] For his success as an intelligence office during the war, Gade was awarded the Navy Cross.

Immediately after the war, the State Department sent Gade to Finland and the new Baltic republics, which were caught between the collapsing German empire and the Bolshevik revolution in Russia. Although officially a diplomat, he described his duties as "principally intelligence service," collecting information on the new Soviet state from secret agents in the Baltic countries and Russia. He early understood that Bolshevik ambitions included subverting not only European countries but also the United States, and after he returned to New York, he wrote a series of articles warning of the communist threat to Western democracy. He also tried to encourage both the US Army and Navy intelligence services to cooperate with each other, going so far as to recommend a "national intelligence service" to receive all intelligence produced by all American agencies, analyze that information, and share it within the government. Neither the army nor the navy was interested, and their stubborn reluctance to cooperate would cost the United States dearly in December 1941.[16]

By the 1930s American intelligence organizations were again wasting away, just as Fascists were seizing control of Germany and Italy, militaristic imperialists were dominating Japan, and the Communist Soviet Union was aggressively planting spies and agitators all over the world. In 1933 a college classmate of Gade's was appointed ambassador to Belgium, and although he was almost sixty years old, Gade agreed to return to Europe as naval attaché to Belgium and the Netherlands.[17] From that vantage point, he watched growing German aggressiveness in re-arming and re-occupying the Rhineland, Austria, and Sudeten portion of Czechoslovakia while communists and Nazis fought for dominance in the Spanish Civil War. Gade tried to encourage both the Dutch and the Belgians to strengthen their intelligence services, as he had fruitlessly attempted earlier to encourage American military intelligence chiefs to cooperate. Having begun his service as a naval intelligence officer working with Scandinavian partners against imperial Germany, Gade ended that service at the age of sixty-five in 1940, as he watched Nazi German armies march into Brussels.

A month later, in June 1940, a much younger naval intelligence colleague, forty-three-year-old Saint Louis native Commander Roscoe Hillenkoetter, watched another victorious German army occupy Paris. Too young for service in World War I, Hillenkoetter—born on May 8, 1897, to Alexander and Olinde Deuker Hillenkoetter, both of whom were also born in Saint Louis—grew up in a working-class German family. His grandfathers were firemen and blacksmiths, his father, Alexander, a career post office mail carrier. Roscoe was appointed to the United States Naval Academy in 1916, and the 1917 Saint Louis Gould's city directory lists him as a "midshipman" at his parents' home at 4147 Green Lea Place, between O'Fallon and Fairgrounds Parks in north Saint Louis.[18] Although he lived at that address only during his high school years, Green Lea Place remained his official military "home of record" until his retirement decades later.[19] Hillenkoetter graduated with distinction from the United States Naval Academy in 1919 and spent his early years as a naval officer serving on surface ships and submarines, and as a staff aide to senior commanders.

First Classman Roscoe H. Hillenkoetter, United States Naval Academy, 1919 (USNA, *Lucky Bag 1920*, 168, courtesy of H. Keith Melton).

After two years teaching modern Romance languages at the naval academy, and more sea duty in cruisers and destroyers, in 1933 he was appointed assistant naval attaché in Paris. Before embarking on that glamorous assignment, at the age of thirty-six, he married the twenty-year-old Philadelphia-born daughter of navy physician Captain G. F. Clark. Jane Clark Hillenkoetter, known as "Janie," accompanied Roscoe on this two-year diplomatic tour, and in September 1935[20] the couple sailed back to the United States, giving Captain Clark's quarters at the naval hospital in Chelsea, Massachusetts, as their temporary address.[21]

Like President Woodrow Wilson during the First World War, President Franklin D. Roosevelt tended to rely upon his personal staff in matters involving foreign intelligence. Unfortunately, the president's personal interest did not always lead to successful collection activities, especially when rival government agencies were involved. For example, while Roosevelt was "delighted at the idea" of assistant Paris naval attaché Hillenkoetter acting as a diplomatic courier traveling to Berlin, Warsaw, Moscow, and Prague as an excuse to observe military facilities, the navy decided that it would be illegal for the State Department to pay his expenses.[22] The navy also decided that after his promising service as an intelligence officer, Hillenkoetter should return to sea, and from October 1935 to February 1938, he was stationed on the battleship *Maryland* in the Pacific. His bride, Jane, as the daughter of a naval officer, was used to long separations, and they managed to spend enough time together that a month after Commander Hillenkoetter left *Maryland*, their daughter Jane was born on March 13, 1938, in Newport, Rhode Island.[23]

A month later in April 1938 he and his young family were back in Paris. This time Hillenkoetter had additional responsibility for Madrid and Lisbon. The American ambassador to Paris, William C. Bullitt, was pleased to have Hillenkoetter join his staff and, in a letter to a senior State Department official, called him "one of the most remarkable young men that I know."[24]

Ambassador William Bullitt in Paris (National Archives College Park, RG306-NT, Box 25c-25, courtesy of the *New York Times* Paris Bureau).

Given the global environment of the late 1930s, with both Germany and Japan already embarked upon aggressive and militaristic expansion threatening all their regional neighbors, it is remarkable how few resources the United States devoted to diplomatic, military, and intelligence activities. In the words of intelligence scholar David Alvarez, "In the two decades following the First World War, the United States claimed the status of a great power but maintained the intelligence resources of a minor power."[25] In 1938 the United States Army had only 69 people in its Military Intelligence Division (MID). At the outbreak of war in Europe in September 1939, the Office of Naval Intelligence(ONI) had 63 people at its Washington headquarters, with only 17 attachés worldwide. Only 9 of these attachés were serving in Europe.[26] Even the State Department, which is, after all, principally responsible for international affairs, had only 683 officers worldwide, with an additional 1,600 clerks and 1,300 other employees. Indeed, according to Hillenkoetter's Foreign Service colleague Douglas MacArthur II, in 1938 when Congress passed a law allowing for a military draft in case of need, an "OHIO" movement arose in the United States, where young men threated to go "Over the Hill in October" rather than serve. As MacArthur noted, "For those of us serving in Europe then, [war] was just a question of when it was going to come."[27]

These were very turbulent years, and both Hillenkoetter in Paris and his senior colleague Captain Gade in Brussels were very active, especially in observing combat in the Spanish Civil War. For European military experts, the American Civil War had been a wonderful laboratory demonstration in industrial mass warfare, and the Spanish Civil War offered American officers early exposure to twentieth-century technological war. In his memoirs, Gade talks about visiting Portugal and Spain, where he observed the German Air Force practicing the tactics that soon would give the German military such easy victories in Poland and Western Europe. He met with French Marshal Philippe Pétain, then ambassador to Spain, and in March 1939 was invited to join the French embassy staff in watching General Francisco Franco enter Madrid and review his own victorious army and his German and Italian allies.[28] Gade, reluctant to be seen at a Fascist celebration, declined the invitation on the grounds that he didn't have a suitable uniform, and just over a year later Hillenkoetter would use a similarly flimsy excuse when invited to join the German general review his victorious troops marching into Paris.

With the victory of Franco's nationalists in Spain and the collapse of his opponents, American citizens, diplomats, journalists, and anti-Franco Spaniards were evacuated from the war zone by American and other Western warships. The *New York Times* reported that "Spanish Insurgent bombers" attacked the Spanish harbor of Caldetas, near Barcelona, and American naval officers said that although the American cruiser *Omaha* illuminated her Stars and Stripes with a searchlight, "projectiles and shell fragments were raining on us, and we thought for a while we would bring some of them back in our pockets."[29] The bombing of the town was particularly fierce, with estimates of hundreds of casualties, but instead of escaping by ship, Lieutenant Commander Hillenkoetter and Lisbon army attaché Lieutenant Colonel Henry Cheadle left the city by car so that they could better evaluate bomb damage and observe the activities of Franco's forces. Hillenkoetter's detailed reporting of the fall of Barcelona included descriptions of the "appalling destruction" caused by Fascist bombers.[30]

Beyond physical courage, self-confidence and boldness are essential traits for military officers, diplomats, and intelligence officers. Ambassador Bullitt was a particularly aggressive officer, and years later Hillenkoetter remembered an episode that occurred shortly after his dramatic escape from the bombing of Barcelona. The FBI told the embassy in Paris that a blond German beauty parlor operator was suspected of being a spy but had managed to escape New York on a German steamship before she could be arrested. Since the ship would stop in the French port of Cherbourg, Bullitt and Hillenkoetter fabricated an "imposing looking" fake arrest warrant, and Hillenkoetter was dispatched to Cherbourg while the new American liner *United States* delayed its departure to take the spy back to New York. The French police immediately recognized the warrant as a fake but agreed "if our blonde disembarked . . . even if only for a walk" they would arrest her and turn her over to Hillenkoetter. "By the time anybody, meaning the Germans, complained, she would be on her way back to the United States." In the end, the woman never left the ship "but we got 'A' for effort and it was so characteristic of [Ambassador Bullitt] to try to get the right solution in a difficult and involved situation."[31]

Ambassador Bullitt and his assistant, Robert Murphy, were both convinced that European war would directly threaten the United States, but France appeared paralyzed in the face of German aggression, first in annexing Austria in March 1938 and then in seizing the German Sudeten region from Czechoslovakia. In July 1938, in the midst of a Czech war scare, Hillenkoetter surveyed Germany's western border defenses by driving from the North Sea southward along the Mosel and Rhine Rivers. "South of the Rhine . . . the country is saturated with troops, aviation fields are numerous and labor battalions are everywhere."

Aside from what he could observe from the road, he picked up hitchhiking labor corps "boys" and soldiers and "by the aid of a few cigarettes and mentioning that we were '*Amerikaner*,'" got the Germans to describe the depth of their fortifications and tank traps. Shortly after his trip, the Germans closed the border area to all attachés and even retired military officers.[32] In September 1938, at a Paris dinner for military attachés, the German officers present expressed annoyance

German Labor Corps "boys," 1935 (Personal collection of Richard E. Schroeder, photographed by Professor A. E. Schroeder).

that the United States was supporting British and French resistance to Adolf Hitler's Sudeten threats. Still, they predicted that war between Germany and the United States would only occur if the United States sent an army to Europe. According to Hillenkoetter's chief, the embassy naval attaché, Captain Francis Cogswell, "[The Germans] were sure we would never do that again, implying that they could act as they wished in Europe regardless of the opinion of the U.S."[33] As the Sudeten crisis continued in the fall of 1938, naval attachés reported that "the exodus from Paris continues" as a renewed war scare gripped France.[34]

Hillenkoetter had a "long personal talk" with the German military attaché, Lieutenant General Erich von Kuhlenthal, who said the Germans and French should form a "continental block" excluding Great Britain. The German naval attaché gave Hillenkoetter the same message. The Americans also collected secret French naval documents and codebooks from cooperative naval and intelligence officers,[35] and in December 1938 Hillenkoetter reported the pessimistic opinion of a French diplomat: "England's help against Germany cannot be counted on too strongly, because it may be lacking, in spite of all agreements, at the critical moment."[36] Beyond the documents provided by the French, the attaché office reported that "the ex-German military attaché has allowed [Hillenkoetter] to copy" a detailed table of organization of the German army as of December 1, 1938,[37] which Hillenkoetter used to write a detailed description of that army less than a year before it destroyed Poland and threatened France.

New Wehrmacht mechanized artillery, 1937 (Personal collection of Richard E. Schroeder, photographed by Professor A. E. Schroeder).

In general, the reporting and analysis that the naval attachés in Paris sent back to the Office of Naval Intelligence was as detailed and sophisticated as that of the State Department diplomats with whom they served, and was not limited to strictly military subjects. Weekly political and international commentaries, many written by Hillenkoetter, were faithfully sent to Washington, and the report on the July 14, 1939, Bastille Day celebration described a huge military display by French forces and their British allies. The report also noted that ongoing Franco-Russian treaty negotiations were "furnishing the Russians with many laughs" amid rumors of a secret German-Russian treaty.[38] In fact that so-called Molotov-Ribbentrop Pact was revealed on August 23, 1939, and included secret protocols dividing Poland between Russia and Germany, and giving Stalin a free hand in Finland.

In late August 1939 Hillenkoetter sent a message to the chief of naval operations, reporting that German forces were ready to invade Poland and predicting that, in such an attack, Great Britain and France would enter the war.[39] In late December 1939, during the pause after the *Blitzkrieg* attack on Poland—which some called a *Sitzkrieg*—Captain Gade wrote a thoughtful analysis of this "war of nerves." "In a war of nerves, with the Germans having none, the English some, and the French

French refugees flee fighting in northern France, June 3, 1940 (National Archives College Park, RG306-NT, Box 1332, file 24, courtesy of the *New York Times* Paris Bureau).

many . . . is it not logical to believe in German victory? . . . Germany's present inaction is . . . too paradoxical to last long."[40] In the spring of 1940 President Roosevelt dispatched Assistant Secretary of State Sumner Welles to Europe on a peace mission, and the acting ambassador, Murphy, accompanied him to meet French leaders. Both men were shocked at how "inept and unrealistic" they were. As Murphy concluded, "Everybody seemed 'just too tired'" to resist the Germans.[41]

By mid-May, with Holland overwhelmed, Belgium about to fall, and the French government preparing to flee Paris, Ambassador Bullitt decided to remain in the city with Murphy, newly promoted naval attaché Hillenkoetter,[42] and army attaché Colonel Horace H. Fuller.[43] Other members of the embassy staff followed the French government south, and families were also evacuated from the war zone. On the night before the German army reached Paris, Murphy and Hillenkoetter went out for a midnight walk. At the doors to the embassy they encountered the Grand Rabbi of Paris and his wife, who had decided too late to flee the city and now hoped that an American embassy car could take them with the rest of the embassy staff to Bordeaux. Murphy ordered an embassy chauffeur to take them, but the car was turned back at the outskirts of Paris by the German armored divisions now surrounding the city. Murphy wrote, "I never saw the Grand Rabbi again," and he feared he had been killed by the Nazis. As the Americans walked "along the ghostly boulevards that sultry night not a café was open, no lights showed anywhere, we met no one."[44]

Just over four years later, in August 1944, two American intelligence officers stood atop the Arch of Triumph watching the liberation of Paris by Free French tanks and American infantry. One of these officers was David Bruce—European chief of the Office of Strategic Services and later a distinguished American diplomat—and the other the daring American novelist and war correspondent Ernest Hemingway, whose stories about the horrors of the Spanish Civil War had moved so many. Bruce had encountered Hemingway leading a band of French guerrilla fighters and given him an OSS commission on the spot. From the Arch of Triumph, they headed for the famous Ritz hotel, where Hemingway flamboyantly ordered martinis for all his fighters.[45]

Things were much less festive on the morning in June 1940, when German forces entered Paris. Murphy, Hillenkoetter, and Fuller crossed the boulevard from the American embassy to German military headquarters in one of Paris's best hotels to pay a formal call on provisional military governor Major General Bogislav von Studnitz. While they waited for a German military convoy to pass, they were politely approached by a German lieutenant who confirmed they were Americans and then asked, "Can you tell us where we might find a suitable hotel?" Since not only the French government but many citizens had fled in the face of the German occupation, the Americans laughed in surprise and responded: "The whole city seems to be in your possession. It has hundreds of empty hotels. Take your pick." They found von Studnitz and his officers in excellent moods as they drank expensive champagne in their luxury hotel. Von Studnitz had been a German army attaché in Warsaw and assured his visitors that he understood that their duty was to gather intelligence and he was thus quite willing to answer their questions fully and frankly.[46] He confidently predicted that because both the French and British armies were shattered, the war would be over in a few weeks. Hillenkoetter asked how the Germans expected to cross the English Channel, but the general confidently responded that "plans were all made and . . . the war would be over in six weeks."

In fact, the Germans proved so open and friendly that von Studnitz invited Hillenkoetter and Colonel Fuller to join him in reviewing his Eighty-Seventh Infantry Division as they marched into Paris. As Hillenkoetter later remembered:

[We] could easily see how that would look in newsreels, photos, etc—two American officers taking a review with a German general. So we hastily,

German troops entering Paris, June 14, 1940 (National Archives College Park RG208-PP-93-8, Box 10).

but firmly, declined, saying that we didn't feel worthy to share the general's honor; that it was his division and his glory; and that it would be a shame to deprive him of even a share of the glory.[47]

To take advantage of initial German friendliness, Bullitt decided to leave Murphy and the attachés in Paris, where they collected much intelligence from high-ranking German officials to be transmitted back to Washington and shared with the British. Murphy proudly noted, "Paris proved to be one of the best, if not the best, of intelligence centers of Europe at that moment."[48] Because the embassy had destroyed its codes, and all diplomatic telegrams were being read by the Germans, this useful but sensitive information was guarded by embassy staff until they left Paris.

Beyond intelligence collection, the embassy took advantage of early German cooperation in other ways. Murphy had not been able to rescue the Grand Rabbi, who in fact did survive the war, but the German army gave the embassy exit permits to allow not only American and British citizens but hundreds of French to escape German-occupied France. Finally, at the end of June 1940 Ambassador

Bullitt, Murphy, Foreign Service clerk Carmel Offie, Hillenkoetter, and the army attaché—accompanied by a British couple carrying fake American passports—drove in a five-car convoy from Paris through German lines to southern France, where the new French government was being set up. False documents identified the civilians as the ambassador's butler and maid, but a border guard complained that the lady was too well-dressed to be a maid. "'Of course not,' Offie piped up, never at a loss. 'Don't you understand that the ambassador has a mistress.'"[49]

The French government was in complete disarray, but the greatest concern shared by President Roosevelt and British Prime Minister Winston Churchill was the fate of the powerful French fleet, most of whose ships were in the Mediterranean. Neither the United States nor Great Britain wanted these warships to be taken over by the German Navy. Churchill's decision in early July to seize or destroy the French fleet at its bases in Egypt and Mers-el-Kébir, Algeria, killing or wounding some two thousand French sailors, almost drove France away from its British ally. The American embassy worked hard to persuade the Vichy government that since the United States had no intention of entering the war, France's only hope was a British victory. Hillenkoetter, as naval attaché, had primary responsibility for working with Admiral François Darlan, Vichy's naval minister, and although Darlan was furious at the British attack, "[Hillenkoetter] used every persuasion on Darlan to prevent his anger from running away with him and soon he agreed to renew his pledge to the American government to keep out of German control what was left of the French fleet."[50] Indeed, in 1942 the surviving French fleet was scuttled by its crews in Toulon, France, to keep the ships out of German hands. The strain between the former French and British allies was intense, with American diplomats caught in the middle. In early September, a dispatch from Vichy to naval intelligence in Washington recounted many of the same French grievances that led the United States to declare war against Great Britain in 1812: the blockade of France and the capture of ships and citizens. The Vichy government was also unhappy that the British were harboring the "illegal government of former general [Charles] de Gaulle."[51] Hillenkoetter's colleague in Madrid was approached by the local French naval attaché seeking a meeting with his British counterpart to offer that Vichy would maintain the French fleet in Toulon "in readiness for action on behalf of England" if the Royal Navy would allow food shipments to France. The American attaché discounted the overture as nothing more than a ploy to get food relief but said the French were considering moving their government from Vichy to French Senegal if German occupation became too harsh.[52]

Trying to calm the furious French admiral, who felt betrayed by Churchill, was undoubtedly the most difficult diplomatic challenge facing a relatively young and inexperienced naval attaché, but Hillenkoetter had other duties as well. In early August he was again mentioned in the *New York Times,* as on his third attempt he managed to deliver diplomatic pouches from the embassy in Vichy to the US embassy in Paris, despite German army insistence that he needed the permission of German occupation authorities. Again, boldness and persistence paid off.[53]

Much more important to the course of the war, however, was a brief trip Hillenkoetter made to French North African countries Morocco and Algeria. While the Vichy government seemed paralyzed by defeat and despair, Murphy reported that Hillenkoetter

> was agreeably surprised and encouraged. . . . Contrary to rumors . . . from London, he found that the Nazis had left French Africa almost completely to its own devices . . . practically the same as before the war. Furthermore, the [French] military . . . was far stronger than he had expected. . . . Hillenkoetter added that these experienced army, navy, and air force officers and men had not lost their . . . fighting spirit. . . . "The atmosphere over there is not comparable to the confusion in Vichy" Hillenkoetter told us. "If France is going to fight again anywhere in this war, I believe North Africa will be the place." He impressed us all with his hopefulness, which was reflected in the reports our Vichy Embassy sent to Washington.

Shortly thereafter Murphy was summoned back to Washington. President Roosevelt had carefully read Hillenkoetter's North African reports and dispatched Murphy to French North Africa as his personal representative.[54]

In September 1940, with Western Europe in German hands, the Battle of Britain raging, German bombs falling on London, and Churchill rallying his countrymen and appealing to the United States for help, Hillenkoetter reported on a conversation with his former German naval attaché colleague from Paris. As good summer flying weather and suitable weather for cross-Channel landing operations were ending, so was initial German confidence in early and easy victory. The Germans could not understand why Great Britain had not surrendered:

> [The Germans] are in the position of a prize fighter who hits his opponent with all his strength in what presumably is a vulnerable spot and yet the opponent won't go down. . . . The failure of England to realize, according to the German viewpoint, that she is beaten leaves the Germans a bit perplexed.

Beyond that, Hillenkoetter observed that his "German acquaintances and friends" were worried about the United States entering the war and angry that Roosevelt had given Churchill fifty old American destroyers to defend British convoys and blockade the European continent. The former German attaché admitted the blockade was hurting them and that German Ford automotive plants building vehicles for the German military were only working at 35 percent capacity. The German gloomily predicted that all of Europe would suffer a hard and hungry winter.[55] Hillenkoetter concluded by noting that the Germans were expressing their unhappiness with the United States in petty ways, in "any transaction of whatever kind between the [American] Embassy and German offices."

At the end of December 1940, a new ambassador replaced Bullitt in Vichy. Admiral William Leahy, born in Hampton, Iowa, in 1875, had retired as chief of naval operations in 1939 and was governor of Puerto Rico when Roosevelt recalled him to try to keep the French, many of whom now felt that England had abandoned and betrayed them, from actively helping Germany. Commander Hillenkoetter met Leahy and his wife in Lisbon, and after a harrowing journey across war-torn Spain, Leahy met with Marshal Philippe Pétain and Admiral François Darlan. Although Darlan was very friendly, Leahy judged him "incurably anti-British" and "prejudiced beyond convincing."[56]

Indeed, he told Leahy that "he had asked the Germans to seize Gibraltar and bomb the Suez Canal, in order to destroy British power in the Mediterranean."[57] Nonetheless, when Dwight Eisenhower's American army invaded North Africa in November 1942, Admiral Darlan, by then commander in chief of French forces, eventually ordered them to join the allies, and his order was obeyed.

During their time in Vichy, Leahy and his wife formed warm friendships with Hillenkoetter and embassy third secretary, Douglas MacArthur II, whose father, Arthur, was a naval academy graduate and friend, and whose uncle was General Douglas MacArthur.[58]

Indeed, as a child, MacArthur had called the formidable Leahy "Uncle Bill." Although embassy staff tried to maintain normal social and diplomatic activities, life in Vichy was extremely stressful. This must have been particularly so for Hillenkoetter, who, beyond his very demanding professional duties, also had to be concerned for his young wife and toddler daughter in an environment of overcrowding and wartime privation.[59] MacArthur came from a family of distinguished soldiers and sailors, and in 1934 had married Laura Louise Barkley, the daughter of Kentucky senator Alben Barkley, who would become Harry Truman's vice president in 1949. Both Laura MacArthur, whom the Hillenkoetters called "Wahwee," and Janie Hillenkoetter had small daughters, and Laura

Admiral François Darlan, Vichy minister of marine, with Nazi officials in Berchtesgaden, Germany (National Archives College Park, 242-JRB 50-67).

"Mimi" MacArthur and Jane "Jay Jay" Hillenkoetter were playmates.[60] Because of German espionage, all sensitive reporting had to be dispatched to Washington by very infrequent and slow couriers. Embassy officers took great care not to maintain written records or diaries because they expected the Germans to, in MacArthur's words, "grab us . . . and any diaries, books, or papers" to try to identify French patriots in touch with the embassy.[61] There was little they could do about their ambassador's habit of recording daily events, and Leahy's diary became the basis for his postwar memoirs.

Ambassador William Leahy and staff, Vichy France, January 8, 1941, with Third Secretary Douglas MacArthur II (*third from right*) and Naval Attaché Commander Roscoe Hillenkoetter (*second from right*) (Harry S. Truman Presidential Library, 67-0001).

One of Hillenkoetter's most interesting and sensitive reports came in July 1941, when a French source gave him the French General Staff analysis of Franco-British cooperation during the spring 1940 Battle of France. Hillenkoetter, who was a certified interpreter of French, Spanish, and German,[62] produced a sophisticated translation of the entire report, which concluded: "When the German drive . . . began, cooperation became lamentable; even ill-will was apparent. Days went by when one side didn't know what the other was up to, and vice versa." In his commentary, Hillenkoetter noted the difficulties in trying to get allies to cooperate, even if both have the best of intentions. He quoted a French general on why the Germans were so militarily successful: "They have no allies." Finally, he praised the French for their rigorous objectivity and harsh self-criticism, commenting that his French source warned, "Here is a very valuable lesson to be learned. For goodness sake, when America comes into the war, don't make the foolish mistakes we did."[63]

Embassy telephones were tapped by both Vichy and German agents, and US embassy officers were followed. One young diplomat wryly noted, "Foreign ladies of a type never to have noticed me in the past, in fact of a type to have avoided me, now find me irresistible."[64] Six years later, as Hillenkoetter, now a rear admiral with the French Legion of Honor award, returned to Washington to take up duty as Director of Central Intelligence, the *Washington Post* described his secret activities in Vichy:

> Hillenkoetter was a familiar figure in the lobbies and bars of the fabulous Hotel Les Ambassadeurs in Vichy after the fall of France . . . he served as a link in the "underground railway" through which thousands of Frenchmen, British and Americans got out of occupied France and the Continent to join the fight against Hitler. Les Ambassadeurs—often called the "international monkey-house"—was his headquarters. It was also the hangout of most of Europe's spies, diplomats and counter-intelligence agents. Hunted men sidled up to him at the bar. During an apparently aimless conversation they received identification papers, gasoline permits, money or a rendezvous with an innocent-appearing truck heading for the border.[65]

There was great concern that Germany might finally occupy Vichy France and even overthrow its Spanish ally General Franco to seize control of the British outpost of Gibraltar and thus the Mediterranean Sea. The embassy, therefore, plotted escape routes and hid supplies of gasoline in buried tin cans along the way, so embassy staff could, if necessary, escape in their cars.[66] Leahy was viciously attacked by the German-controlled French press, "Combining Anglo-Saxon hypocrisy with Jewish rapacity, this Admiral was performing a task that we ordinarily confide to secret emissaries called spies."[67]

Embassies, of course, did house intelligence officers, and eventually Commander Hillenkoetter received a new assistant naval attaché, a young Chicago lawyer named Thomas Cassady. Leahy remarked:

> I soon found he did not know which end of a boat went first and wondered what kind of officers the Navy was commissioning. Some time later, I learned he was a secret OSS agent planted in the American Embassy. Cassady was a very good spy—capable and discreet. He succeeded so well in keeping his secret that when the Embassy staff was imprisoned by the Germans in November 1942 the Nazis could not make a case against him although they definitely suspected espionage.

As Leahy admitted, "I did not know either [Office of Strategic Services director William J.] Donovan or the OSS. . . . We learned later of their efficiency in collecting and evaluating intelligence about Axis military and political plans."[68] Leahy respected Hillenkoetter's skill in helping French underground members escape to North Africa and in collecting information from both French and German sources. Like Cassady, "He never got caught."[69] Unfortunately, while Hillenkoetter and his family returned to the United States in the summer of 1941, both MacArthur and Cassady remained at the Vichy embassy and in November 1942 were interned in Germany after the Allied invasion of North Africa. MacArthur was treated correctly, but Cassady was brutally tortured by the German *Gestapo* to try to get him to identify his French Resistance contacts. Both MacArthur and Cassady remained in Germany until 1944, after which MacArthur became one of the first State Department diplomats to return to Paris in August 1944, as the Allies liberated the city.[70] By that time, as President Roosevelt's representative on the Joint Chiefs of Staff, Leahy was part of the senior military leadership to whom the OSS reported.

Meanwhile, in French North Africa, Robert Murphy was acting as Roosevelt's representative. There were five American consulates throughout the French territories, and Murphy made a secret agreement with French authorities under which twelve new vice-consuls could be assigned to these posts and use secret codes and diplomatic pouches to report back to Washington. Unfortunately, since the State Department did not have enough specialized staff, it occurred to Assistant Secretary of State Adolf Berle "that what were needed were experienced Army and Navy officers, brave, patriotic, disciplined men who could appreciate objects and events of military significance." To Murphy's disappointment, "Our Intelligence organization . . . was primitive and inadequate. It was timid, parochial, and operating strictly in the tradition of the Spanish-American War." The Navy's Office of Naval Intelligence (ONI) and Army's Military Intelligence Division (MID) were reluctant to help the State Department but eventually nominated a group with some knowledge of French but none of the Arabic language or Muslim countries. The Germans quickly became aware of these men and reported to Berlin: "We can only congratulate ourselves on the selection of this group of enemy agents who will give us no trouble. In view of the fact that they are totally lacking in method, organization, and discipline, the danger presented by their arrival in North Africa [is] nil." While Murphy thought this German assessment a gross exaggeration, he told Washington that "one or two of us, with luck, might be able to distinguish a battleship from a submarine on a particularly clear day."[71] After their early service as Murphy's vice-consuls, many continued their wartime intelligence service as OSS officers.

According to Murphy, Roosevelt had given Donovan's OSS:

> plenty of money to create the kind of spy-subversive secret service long employed by European powers but previously scorned by Americans. The

American army and navy had consistently down-graded their Intelligence sections, and Donovan proposed now to fill the gap. We surely were glad to welcome his representatives.[72]

Donovan's chief African representative was US Marine Colonel William A. Eddy, who had grown up in the Middle East, was fluent in Arabic, had a PhD from Princeton University, and had served as president of Hobart College in Geneva, New York. A decorated veteran of World War I—where he had lost a leg—Eddy's combat medals and "noticeable limp" inspired salty General George Patton to observe, "The son of a bitch's been shot at enough, hasn't he?"[73] Based in Tangier as the naval attaché, he was "always meticulous in coordinating his activities with [Murphy's] and no American knew more about Arabs or about power politics in Africa."

Departing Ambassador William Leahy (*right*) and Vichy chief of state Marshal Philippe Pétain, April 27, 1942 (Naval History and Heritage Command, NH 89478).

In June of 1941 Germany invaded Russia, and in the fall, Japan took French Indochina. By then Commander Hillenkoetter had been recalled to the United States, arriving in New York on September 15, 1941, with his wife and three-year-old daughter on the Pan American Yankee Clipper from Lisbon. On November 14, 1941, he arrived in Honolulu without his family to take up his duties as executive officer, or second-in-command, of the battleship *West Virginia* at Pearl Harbor.[74] Another Missourian, Commander Samuel Fuqua, was Executive Officer on *Arizona*.[75] Leahy remained in Vichy until the unexpected death of his wife in April 1942, after which he escorted her body back to the United States.

He resigned as ambassador on July 18, 1942, and two days later Roosevelt recalled him to active military duty as Chief of Staff to the Commander in Chief of the United States Army and Navy, a position he held for both Presidents Roosevelt and Truman for the next seven years.

America in World War II
and the Beginnings of Central Intelligence

I<small>F MOST ASPECTS OF THE</small> American intelligence effort fell well behind the country's rivals and enemies after World War I, the United States did have remarkable success in the field of communications intelligence or code-breaking—especially against Japan. In the Washington Naval Conference of 1922, the World War I Western Allies tried to prevent another ruinous naval arms race like the competition between imperial Germany and Great Britain before 1914. The United States and Great Britain were alarmed by growing Japanese aggressiveness following Japan's shocking destruction of the Russian fleet in 1905 and wanted to limit the size of the Japanese fleet relative to the size of the American and British battle fleets. The United States was successful in limiting the number of Japanese battleships because brilliant American code-breaker Herbert Yardley could read Japan's diplomatic telegrams that laid out its negotiating strategy.[1] In September 1940, the same month that the British broke the famous German "Enigma" cipher machine, US Army analysts began reading what US code-breakers called Japan's "Purple" diplomatic machine.[2] The British called the Enigma messages ULTRA, while the Americans used the code word MAGIC for decoded Japanese material. Unhappily, despite the reach of American radio intercept stations, and the skill of American military code-breakers, the national effort was muddled by bitter rivalry between the American navy and army, which refused to cooperate until forced to do so. Beyond that rivalry, the Japanese messages were so secret that only the most senior Washington officials—including President Roosevelt and the secretaries of state, war, and the navy—saw them. As William J. Casey, a senior OSS officer who later became President Ronald Reagan's director of central intelligence, said: "The military had confined the priceless intercepts to a handful of people too busy to interpret them. . . . No one had put the pieces together . . . and told [senior officials] of their momentous implications."[3]

Among the first to suffer the consequences of America's feeble intelligence apparatus were Commander Hillenkoetter and the sailors of the Pacific Fleet on Sunday, December 7, 1941. The captain of *West Virginia*, Mervyn Bennion, was mortally wounded early in the attack, and executive officer Hillenkoetter was trapped by fierce fires sparked by the explosion of *Arizona* as well as by the more than half dozen torpedoes and bombs that struck his ship.[4]

West Virginia ablaze at Pearl Harbor (National Archives College Park, RG80-G, Box 91, photo 19930).

Thanks to the heroism and skill of her crew, *West Virginia* was saved from capsizing, but settled to the bottom of the shallow harbor with relatively light loss of life as her surviving crew continued to fight raging fires. The next day, on orders from Admiral Walter Anderson, who as director of naval intelligence had been Hillenkoetter's boss when he served as attaché in Paris in 1940, Hillenkoetter sent two sailors to hoist an American flag over the ruins of *Arizona*.[5]

Both Commander Samuel Fuqua of *Arizona* and Captain Bennion of *West Virginia* received Medals of Honor at Pearl Harbor, while Hillenkoetter, also wounded, only received a Purple Heart. A black mess attendant, Doris "Dorie"

Miller, who helped defend *West Virginia* and evacuate the wounded, was awarded the Navy's third-highest honor, the Navy Cross, in May 1942 by Admiral Chester Nimitz, Commander in Chief of the Pacific Fleet. Within a week of the Japanese attack, Hillenkoetter was appointed executive officer of *Maryland*, whose crew worked around the clock to make quick repairs, allowing the battleship to support the decisive Battle of Midway in early June 1942, which fatally crippled Japan's naval air forces.[6]

Finally, in September 1942, newly promoted Captain Hillenkoetter was given one of the most important, but also most controversial, intelligence assignments in the navy, when he was appointed chief of intelligence for Admiral Nimitz.[7] Hillenkoetter's new office grew from one of the navy's string of Pacific radio-intercept and direction-finding stations used to locate the positions of Japanese warships and try to listen to their communications. The Japanese had been emboldened by their victory over Russia in 1905 and were angry and resentful that American code-breakers had forced them to accept the humiliating battleship limitations of the Washington Naval Conference of 1922. The Japanese knew of this intelligence success because Herbert Yardley boasted about this triumph in his book *The American Black Chamber,* published in 1931 after moralistic Secretary of State Henry Stimson had shut down American code-breaking in 1929.[8] Yardley's book was widely read in Japan, but fortunately for the United States, despite Japanese efforts to protect its secrets during World War II, American code-breakers repeatedly gave American leaders insight into Japan's secrets.

In the 1930s the militaristic Japanese government set out on an aggressive expansionist course. It annexed Manchuria and brutally attacked China. Like Germany at the same time, Japan also energetically built up its military forces while trying to conceal its new strength. The country limited the freedom of foreign, especially American and British, military attachés and went so far as to erect screens around its shipyards to hide the construction of what was to be the world's biggest battleship: *Yamato.* Well aware of the Japanese threat, and eager to keep close watch on the imperial navy, the United States Navy established radio posts in the Philippines, on the Pacific islands of Guam, Samoa, Midway, and Hawaii, and as far north as Dutch Harbor, Alaska.[9] Over the vast distances of the Pacific Ocean, the only way to locate ships was for several stations to hear their radio transmissions and then triangulate their location, and continuing to listen to establish their course and speed. Several of these stations, including Cast in the Philippines and Hypo in Hawaii, were also staffed with code-breakers, who worked with naval code-breaking headquarters in Washington to break Japanese naval codes. Unfortunately, the work on the Japanese Purple diplomatic codes was carried out only in Washington and, as noted by CIA director William Casey, not shared with Hawaii, the American military stronghold first attacked by the Japanese in December 1941. Also, the Japanese navy had carefully prepared for the December attack and kept strict radio silence from the time their aircraft carriers left port until their aircraft appeared over Hawaii. Navy listening posts knew that the Japanese fleet had disappeared into the vast Pacific Ocean but had no idea, or any way of discovering, exactly where it was.

The Japanese believed that the surprise attack on Pearl Harbor, which crippled the American Pacific Fleet, would give them the freedom to overpower all of Southeast Asia and the Pacific Islands, and for months it appeared that they were correct. Guam quickly fell and, after unexpectedly stout resistance, so did Wake Island.[10] The day after Pearl Harbor, Japanese bombers crippled General Douglas MacArthur's Philippine air fleet, the strongest American air forces outside the United States. Two days later Japanese aircraft attacked and destroyed the British battleship *Prince of Wales* near Singapore, the first—but not the last—time that such a powerful ship would be destroyed exclusively by air attack. Just before Christmas, Japanese army forces landed on the main Philippine island of Luzon, and on Christmas Day, Hong Kong fell. Although US Army soldiers hung on stubbornly on Bataan and the island of Corregidor, the personnel of the navy's Cast listening post were moved to safety in Australia. MacArthur escaped on a PT boat with a Medal of Honor for "conspicuous leadership in preparing . . . to resist conquest . . . confirming the faith of the American people in their Armed Forces."[11] The starving survivors of the US Army in the Philippines finally surrendered at Corregidor in early May 1942, just three weeks after army bombers, led by Lieutenant Colonel James "Jimmy" Doolittle, flew off the aircraft carrier *Hornet* and bombed Tokyo in the first dramatic American counterattack—and less than five months after Pearl Harbor.[12] A month after Corregidor came the first great American success of the Pacific war, thanks in large part to the skill of American intelligence officers and the commander who trusted them.

Since May 1941, brilliant code-breaker Joseph Rochefort, one of only fifty navy officers trained to understand Japanese, had commanded the Hawaiian intelligence station Hypo. Officially, Rochefort and Hypo worked for the navy's code-breaking organization in Washington, but Pacific Fleet commander Admiral Husband Kimmel and his fleet intelligence officer, Lieutenant Commander Edwin T. Layton, another Japan expert, looked to Rochefort's local office for overall intelligence support.[13] Indeed, beyond radio interception, Rochefort's newly named Combat Intelligence Unit (CIU) began trying to understand the organization of the Japanese fleet and the capabilities of such dangerous Japanese weapons as the *Zero* fighter plane. Both Layton and Rochefort quickly gained the hostility of their Washington superiors, such as the navy director of war plans,

Captain Joseph J. Rochefort, chief of Intelligence Center, Pacific Ocean Area, Pearl Harbor, Hawaii, 1942 (Naval History and Heritage Command, NH 84826).

Captain—later admiral—Richmond Turner, who felt that his operational planning staff, rather than intelligence officers, should be responsible for analyzing Japanese intentions. Turner and his Washington allies not only withheld access to Japanese MAGIC diplomatic messages, but then blamed Admiral Kimmel and his Hawaii staff for the Pearl Harbor disaster. In his outspoken memoirs, Pearl Harbor intelligence officer Layton described Turner as an "opinionated, stubborn fool" and recounted almost coming to blows with the very senior admiral during the final Japanese surrender in Tokyo Bay in September 1945.[14] Remarkably, while Kimmel was recalled in disgrace in December 1941 and Rochefort himself was later ruined by his jealous Washington navy enemies, Layton continued to serve as fleet intelligence officer for Admiral Nimitz's Pacific Fleet until almost the end of the war.

When Admiral Nimitz took command of the shattered Pacific Fleet in late December, he prudently retained almost all of Admiral Kimmel's staff, including his intelligence officers. Unfortunately, he had few weapons with which to resist the Japanese advance through the Philippines, the South Pacific islands, and across the Pacific Ocean. His battleships were damaged or destroyed, but by a stroke of good fortune, his aircraft carriers had been away from Pearl Harbor on December 7, and he still had Commanders Layton and Rochefort. Nimitz and Chief of Naval Operations Admiral Ernest J. King spent the spring of 1942 planning their counterattack and drawing up the outline for a Pacific Fleet joint intelligence center. The center would collect and analyze photos, maps, and radio intercepts; gather all that information into an authoritative reference database; and then try to estimate Japanese locations, strengths, and intentions. Meanwhile, Rochefort's fifty-person CIU staff worked to locate Japanese warships and, most important, to attack and finally break new high-level Japanese naval codes. Based on this new MAGIC intelligence, Rochefort and Layton persuaded Admiral Nimitz to set a trap for the Japanese fleet by making it appear that the small American garrison on Midway Island was suffering a water shortage. Subsequent Japanese radio messages confirmed that Rochefort had indeed broken their code.[15] In June 1942 Nimitz's aircraft carriers ambushed the unsuspecting and confident Japanese carriers. The Japanese navy would never recover from the loss of those carriers and, even more significant, from the loss of their highly trained and skillful pilots.

A few weeks later, on June 24, 1942, Admiral Nimitz created the Intelligence Center, Pacific Ocean Area, or ICPOA, with Rochefort as commander. Rochefort's original CIU was still responsible for radio interception, direction finding, and code-breaking. The larger center, with some 190 staff, now added sections to analyze captured documents and prisoner interrogation reports as the navy and Marine Corps began retaking Pacific islands, starting with Guadalcanal, which had been captured by the advancing Japanese army. The center also began publishing weekly reports to Washington and the Pacific Fleet so that the officers on the islands and aboard the fighting ships would have the latest intelligence, translations, interrogations, information on Japanese weapons and tactics, and ICPOA's best estimates on the enemy's strength and location. For Rochefort's brilliant contribution to the victory at Midway, Admiral Nimitz nominated him for the Distinguished Service Medal, but Chief of Naval Operations Admiral King, swayed by jealous enemies in Washington who tried to take credit for Midway while blaming Rochefort for missing warning signs before Pearl Harbor, refused him this honor and recalled him from Hawaii. Eventually, this exceptional Japanese linguist, intelligence officer, and code-breaker was assigned as commander of a floating dry dock in San Francisco.[16]

In his place, Captain Roscoe Hillenkoetter was appointed commander, Intelligence Center, Pacific Ocean Area (ICPOA), a position he held from September

1942 until March 1943. In the words of one historian, "Simultaneously dismayed and driven by duty, ICPOA's analysts continued working without their former commander to provide the best intelligence they could for [Nimitz]."[17] Aside from serious morale problems, Hillenkoetter had to deal with many of the same resource problems facing the entire American war effort. New personnel with basic Japanese-language skills would appear, but they would be without necessary analytic skills or experience, which required extensive on-the-job training. Normally, analysts would work fifteen to seventeen hours a day, seven days a week. However, during Hillenkoetter's months, the number of personnel would sometimes not match the workload, and people would be moved to other assignments in a "helter-skelter personnel flow" that hindered the delivery of intelligence to Nimitz.[18] Hillenkoetter did have access to OSS reports, since a small Coordinator of Information (COI) office had been set up in Honolulu a month after Pearl Harbor. The office continued under OSS to provide analytic studies, secret agent reports, and interrogation information to the navy. Admiral Nimitz, on the other hand, never permitted OSS to receive ICPOA information.[19]

With much of Southeast Asia and the southwestern Pacific lost to the triumphant Japanese navy and army, early American and British efforts focused on protecting Australia and supply lines to the United States. After the Philippines fell, the Japanese threatened Port Moresby on the island of New Guinea from their base at Rabaul on New Britain, as well as Allied supply lines from a new airfield the Japanese were building on Guadalcanal in the Solomon Islands. After a brief but bitter dispute between General MacArthur and Admiral King about whether MacArthur or Nimitz should direct the new campaign, US Marines landed on Guadalcanal in early August 1942 and immediately seized the Japanese airfield. For the next six months, each side struggled to send more troops and supplies to the mountainous jungle-covered island, with the American and Japanese fleets clashing repeatedly in bloody duels. While the US Navy was initially at a clear disadvantage, by the time the Japanese abandoned the island in February 1943, the American fleet had proven itself the equal of the Japanese. On shore, the American marines and army soldiers proved equally determined and fierce, while in New Guinea, Australian troops stopped the Japanese advance despite General MacArthur's low opinion of their ability.[20]

Slowly, the war began to produce useful intelligence for Hillenkoetter's analysts. The first Japanese prisoner of war had been Ensign Kazuo Sakamaki, the only survivor from the five midget submarines that participated in the attack on Pearl Harbor. He considered his capture a disgrace, demanded to be shot, and refused to answer any questions. On the other hand, thirty-two sailors from the aircraft carrier *Hiryu*, including the chief engineer, had been abandoned as the carrier sank during the Battle of Midway. An interrogator flown out from ICPOA found them "reasonably cooperative" in disclosing "many facts and details clarifying our knowledge of the battle."[21] In early 1943, according to an ICPOA analyst, US troops on Guadalcanal began capturing a "steady stream" of Japanese personal diaries written in a cursive script that American translators found very challenging. "Japanese soldiers and sailors were addicted to keeping diaries. Some . . . had real literary merit. Sometimes they provided intelligence of considerable value and occasionally they were evidence of war atrocities."[22]

Two analytic successes were particularly important. A map from a crashed Japanese airplane showed the secret code used to designate any geographic location in the world, but it was not until US Marine officer Alva B. Lasswell suggested using a nursery rhyme by which Japanese children learned their language that the code "fell into place like a marine platoon at the bugle's call."[23] In early 1943 ICPOA code-breakers also broke the code used for Japanese supply convoys. Every morning, intelligence analysts would meet with Pacific Fleet submarine planners to compare the movements of Japanese convoys to the current locations of US submarines. According to one scholar of the Pacific war, "There were nights when nearly every American submarine on patrol in the Central Pacific was working on the basis of information derived from [code-breaking]."[24]

In January 1943, at a conference in Casablanca, President Roosevelt and British Prime Minister Churchill agreed that while their first priority would be defeating Nazi Germany and winning the European war, there would be no easing of the pressure on Japan. Unfortunately, the army and navy continued to squabble over Pacific strategy and whether MacArthur or Nimitz should lead the attack. Finally, agreement was reached that General MacArthur, supported by Admiral William F. "Bull" Halsey, Jr., would attack northward from New Guinea and Guadalcanal. Soon, new and more effective American aircraft and tactics were turning the tide in the South Pacific, and with the Japanese increasingly unable to supply or reinforce their troops, Admiral Isoroku Yamamoto, the victor of Pearl Harbor, decided to launch mass waves of inexperienced pilots against Allied positions in New Guinea and Guadalcanal. Their exaggerated reports of success so encouraged the Japanese that Yamamoto decided to visit them, and in mid-April code-breakers in Hawaii decoded the route his airplane would take. Captain Layton, Pacific Fleet intelligence officer, immediately reported the news to Admiral Nimitz, and on April 18, 1943, thanks to MAGIC, Japan's best World War II military commander and strategist was ambushed and killed by US Army fighter planes.[25]

Just a few weeks before this great success by the analysts of the Pacific Fleet's intelligence center, Captain Hillenkoetter had been transferred back to sea duty as commander of the naval destroyer tender *Dixie* in the Solomon Islands, where he served until February 1944.

Hillenkoetter had earned Nimitz's commendation, and OSS chief William Donovan wanted him to take charge of OSS operations in the Pacific, "but the Navy would not release him."[26] During this period, Hillenkoetter also served as the representative of Admiral Nimitz's destroyer commander in the South Pacific, putting Hillenkoetter again in the middle of the strategic competition between General MacArthur and Admiral Nimitz for control of the Pacific theater. Interestingly enough, Hillenkoetter's fellow Missourian Samuel Fuqua of *Arizona* would later command *Dixie* from 1949 to 1950, by which time Hillenkoetter himself was Harry Truman's director of central intelligence.[27] For his service commanding *Dixie*, Hillenkoetter was finally awarded the Bronze Star "for meritorious service."

As Hillenkoetter's successor, army colonel and later brigadier general, Joseph J. Twitty, concluded, the intelligence center's goal was not to produce "'apple

Destroyer tender *Dixie* (AD-14) with its charges (Naval History and Heritage Command, NH 905541).

William J. Donovan's favorite picture of himself as a major in the Sixty-Ninth New York Volunteers during World War I (National Archives College Park, RG226, Box 236, folder 19).

polishing perfection,' but to provide enough intelligence to get the job done."[28] From this perspective, getting the job done meant helping Admiral Nimitz and the troops and sailors under his command in their daily fight against the Japanese, from island to island and over, on, and under the broad Pacific Ocean. The "combat intelligence" Hillenkoetter and then Twitty supplied included information about Japanese forces and their strength, disposition, and probable movements, but necessarily quickly expanded to include detailed data about the islands on which the Americans would fight in their long march to Japan.[29]

More general global information to help the president and his generals and admirals direct the worldwide war was left to ONI in Washington, the Army's Military Intelligence Division, and an ambitious new organization led by dashing World War I Medal of Honor winner William J. Donovan.

William J. Donovan and the
Office of Strategic Services

Historians of Franklin Roosevelt have noted how well suited his management style was to the popular idea of an intelligence chief—for good or bad. "I never let my right hand know what my left hand does . . . . I am perfectly willing to mislead and tell untruths if it will help me win the war." His son James quoted him as saying, "You play the game the way it's been played over the years, and you play to win."[1] He loved to hoard secrets, and "manipulated people, conducted intrigues, scattered responsibility, duplicated assignments, provoked rivalries . . ." To the frustration of his cabinet secretaries, who were responsible for advising him on foreign policy and national defense, Roosevelt delighted in managing his own foreign intelligence network of personal friends, whom he dispatched on private foreign missions, deliberately bypassing ambassadors and the few military attachés stationed overseas. Two of these men were wealthy Philadelphia journalist and novelist William C. Bullitt, "a man of great . . . intellectual energy, and egocentric brilliance" and Irish American college football quarterback, war hero, and prominent Republican New York lawyer William J. Donovan. Even before assuming the presidency in early 1933, Roosevelt sent Bullitt to Europe in violation of the Logan Act, which forbids informal diplomatic activity by private citizens.[2] Despite embarrassing news stories about Bullitt's activities, President Roosevelt appointed him his first ambassador to Moscow and later sent him to Paris, where he and Hillenkoetter worked on such audacious schemes as their effort to use fake documents to capture a suspected German spy after her escape from New York.

Donovan had been assistant US attorney general in the late 1920s and ran unsuccessfully as a Republican to replace Roosevelt as governor of New York when Roosevelt was first elected president in 1932. During the 1930s, he traveled frequently to Europe, meeting Italian dictator Benito Mussolini, observing the

Italian war against Ethiopia, watching German military maneuvers, and even accompanying an attack in the Spanish Civil War. Donovan became close to the British intelligence chief in New York, William "Little Bill" Stephenson, who encouraged senior British officials—including King George VI, Prime Minister Winston Churchill, and Secret Intelligence Service (MI6) chief Stewart Menzies—to receive him in August 1940 after the fall of France to convince both Donovan and Roosevelt that England would continue to fight Hitler but desperately needed American help. Beyond encouraging President Roosevelt's decision to give England fifty old American destroyers, Donovan requested and received many intelligence reports from the British, which were distributed among senior Washington officials. He also supported "full intelligence collaboration" between the United States and Great Britain, which still remains strong more than seventy years later.[3] In December 1940 he was again in Europe and the Mediterranean—including the Balkans, Greece, and Egypt—meeting generals, senior government officials, and kings. As a CIA historian noted:

> Wherever he went he discussed whatever pertained to the winning of the war-strategy, tactics, aircraft, ordnance, transportation, training, health [as well as functions he would include in OSS, such as] intelligence, special operations, psychological warfare, commandos, and guerrilla units.[4]

Donovan was greeted warmly in Washington upon his return in spring 1941 and even broadcast a radio report to the country reporting his conclusions. Not everybody was so enthusiastic, however, and on April 8 the army's chief intelligence officer, Brigadier General Sherman Miles, wrote to General George C. Marshall in alarm:

> There is considerable reason to believe [that Donovan wants] to establish a super agency controlling all intelligence . . . Such an agency, no doubt under Col. Donovan, would collect, collate, and possibly even evaluate all military intelligence . . . . From the point of view of the War Department, such a move would . . . be very disadvantageous, if not [disastrous].[5]

In fact, in 1940 and the early months of 1941, neither the restless Donovan nor the wily president seemed sure how to harness the colonel's energy and enthusiasm. In a decision the army would regret, Secretary of War Henry Stimson rejected his request for command "of the toughest division in the whole [army]."[6] Still, Donovan was obviously giving great thought to how best to organize a strategic national intelligence organization using the British Secret Intelligence Service as a model, and he spelled out his thoughts to his friend and supporter Secretary of the Navy Frank Knox in late April:

[The chief of intelligence operations] should be appointed by the president directly responsible to him and no one else. [He] should have a [secret] fund solely for . . . foreign investigation. [He should have] sole charge of intelligence work abroad, to coordinate the activities of military and naval attachés and others in the collection of information abroad, to . . . interpret all information from whatever source to be available for the president and for such other services as he would designate. [Beyond narrow intelligence functions] interception and inspection . . . of mail and cables; the interception of radio communication; the use of propaganda to penetrate behind enemy lines; the direction of active subversive operations in enemy countries.[7]

Not surprisingly, given the suspicion and hostility of military intelligence organizations—and Roosevelt's own chaotic management style—Donovan never achieved his ideal. However, almost all of these powers eventually came to the director of the postwar national intelligence organization created by Roosevelt's successor, Harry S. Truman.

The Coordinator of Information

Typically, Roosevelt kept his own counsel and toyed with Donovan, even suggesting that he take the job of selling war bonds in New York State.[8] Finally, on June 10, 1941, Donovan and Roosevelt met privately, and the president scrawled a note to "set this up confidentially."[9] Again, Roosevelt left it to others to work out exactly what he meant, but while the Bureau of the Budget and army struggled to define Donovan's new duties, the colonel was already bringing his new office into existence. On July 11, 1941, with the Battle of Britain over, the Atlantic U-boat war in full swing, the Japanese in China and Southeast Asia, and Germany two weeks into its surprise invasion of Hitler's former ally Russia, Roosevelt finally signed the order designating Donovan "Coordinator of Information" to "collect and analyze all information and data, which may bear upon national security . . . and to make such information . . . available to the president . . . . And to carry out, when requested by the president . . . supplemental activities." The order directed the rest of the government to give the COI "all and any such information" as Donovan, with Roosevelt's approval, requested.[10]

Within days Donovan had offices in the new Federal Triangle "Apex Building" closest to the Capitol; was talking to the Librarian of Congress, the famous poet

Brigadier General William Donovan, Director, Office of Strategic Services, in his office on "Navy Hill," Foggy Bottom, Washington, DC (National Archives College Park, RG226, Box 236, folder 19).

Archibald MacLeish, about organizing and housing his new research staff of distinguished university professors and other experts; and was recruiting staff from his years at the Department of Justice and from elite New York law firms, Wall Street investment houses, and banks. Within a few weeks, he moved his headquarters into the old navy medical buildings near George Washington University, directly across the street from the site of the post-World War II State Department building, now named for Harry Truman. He also requested an initial budget of $10 million, more than six times what the Bureau of the Budget thought he would need for COI's first year. Demonstrating Donovan's ambition, his 1942 budget request was $75 million.

Donovan envisioned a large organization with many functions, although he lost many bureaucratic battles to his implacable Washington enemies. As two OSS veterans remembered, these other institutions—principally the FBI, State Department, army, and navy—"forgot their . . . animosities and joined in an attempt to strangle this unwanted newcomer at birth."[11]

Close-up of OSS and CIA headquarters on Navy Hill, north of the Lincoln Memorial (National Archives College Park, RG18AA, Box 146, 32154 A.C., August 30, 1946, US Army Air Corps).

The OSS War Report, written in 1946 at Admiral William D. Leahy's request, noted, "[After Pearl Harbor] . . . many in Washington who did not believe they knew exactly what should be done, at least thought they knew what someone else should be prevented from doing." After the war, they would again try to kill Harry Truman's new CIA.[12]

Once the United States entered World War II, the country's military leadership structure evolved to meet the burdens of global war. By mid-1942, the war was being managed by a Joint Chiefs of Staff, or JCS, consisting of Army Chief of Staff General George C. Marshall, Chief of Naval Operations Admiral Ernest J. King, US Army Air Force commander Lieutenant General Henry H. Arnold, and military chief of staff to the president and former ambassador to France Admiral Leahy.[13] To defend his new organization from its Washington enemies, Donovan turned to Brigadier General Walter Bedell Smith, secretary of the JCS. The brilliant but irascible Beetle Smith went on to become the indispensable chief of staff to Supreme Allied Commander General Dwight Eisenhower during the conquest of Western Europe, and in 1950, he replaced Hillenkoetter as second director of the new Central Intelligence Agency. President Roosevelt agreed to the transfer of most COI functions to the newly created OSS under the JCS on June 13, 1942, with Donovan as director of strategic services. The very brief order creating the OSS said only that the new organization would "collect and analyze . . . strategic information . . . [and] plan and operate such special services as may be directed by the United States Joint Chiefs of Staff."[14] Saint Louis lawyer Clark Clifford—who, as President Truman's naval aide and White House counsel, would later play a major role in the creation of the postwar Defense Department and CIA—called the OSS "the most romantic of all wartime organizations."[15]

The OSS lost COI's foreign propaganda function to a new Office of War Information; was never allowed to operate in Latin America, which J. Edgar Hoover considered FBI territory; and never gained the commando or ranger capability so dear to Donovan's heart. On the other hand, the analytic Research and Analysis (R&A) unit of the OSS flourished. Using the model of the Secret Intelligence Service and wartime Special Operations Executive (SOE)—which Winston Churchill ordered to "set Europe ablaze"—the OSS formed a Secret Intelligence (SI) Branch to recruit and manage foreign spies and a Special Operations (SO) Branch to work with SOE, conduct sabotage, and work with local resistance forces to attack German, Italian, and Japanese forces from behind enemy lines.[16] After the war, one early and bitter challenge was to combine these two functions into a single CIA organization, misleadingly called the Directorate of Plans. To arm and equip his officers, Donovan also formed a Research and Development (R&D) branch under the leadership of brilliant chemist and inventor Stanley Lovell. All of Donovan's ideas and functions survived the war and made up the basis for the modern CIA, as did the far-flung network of overseas offices from which OSS officers operated.

Donovan recognized that America's only goal was the destruction of the Axis powers, and he drew his staff from all walks of life and all political views, from communists to rock-ribbed conservatives. His psychological screening staff sought men and women with "freedom from disturbing prejudices . . . or racial intolerance" and, for his frontline personnel, officers with "disciplined daring," who were "calculatingly reckless" and "trained for aggressive action."[17] For training, the OSS turned to its more experienced British cousins— of the Secret Intelligence Service (MI6), Security Service (MI5), and Special Operations Executive,—who, after all, had been fighting the Germans for some time. For the tools of espionage, sabotage, and secret warfare, however, Donovan had his own "Professor Moriarty," so named for the evil criminal genius of Sherlock Holmes's adventures. As Stanley Lovell recalled in his informal and darkly humorous memoirs, he met Donovan in his deserted OSS office one evening. The "pear-shaped," "soft-spoken" Donovan told him:

> I want every subtle device and every underhanded trick to use against the Germans and the Japanese—by our own people—but especially by the underground groups of all occupied countries. You will have to invent all of them, Lovell, because you're going to be my man. Come with me. I had

never met a man of such magnetism. I heard myself say: "I will." He said: "Start tomorrow."[18]

Delighted at the idea of throwing "all your normal law-abiding concepts out the window," Lovell's scientists, forgers, and chemists created a whole catalog of devices—from knives and silenced guns to clandestine radios and codes used by officers like Virginia Hall, to explosives and chemicals for crippling vehicles and engines, to secret cameras and copying devices for reproducing secret enemy documents.[19]

According to Lovell, Donovan took a silenced OSS pistol into the Oval Office and fired the bullets into a sandbag while President Roosevelt sat across the room dictating letters to his secretary, without either Roosevelt or the secretary noticing the shots. As recounted by Lovell, Roosevelt's only comment was "Bill, you're the only . . . Republican I'll ever allow in my office with a weapon like this."[20] Perhaps his most devilish device was a substance with a "violent, repulsive, and lasting odor" that "patriot" Chinese children could squirt on Japanese officers to "create disturbances, attack morale, and divert attention." It was called "Who, Me?"[21]

The Scholars of the OSS

Perhaps most important, for the first time in American history, Donovan's new creation rallied the social science skills housed in the faculties of America's great universities. Critics of Donovan and his OSS accused the organization of being made up of his "Oh so Social" circle of Wall Street bankers and fancy big-city lawyers, but in fact, "Donovan . . . had a high regard for professors, placing them above diplomats, scientists, and even 'lawyers and bankers.'" He loved taking their studies to Roosevelt on his many visits to the White House.[22] For the first time, the president now had a group of highly intelligent and experienced experts free of army, navy, or State Department loyalties, policy preferences, or prejudices, who were able to give Donovan, the president, and other national civilian and military leaders the impartial results of their study and research without having to defer to the policy positions of cabinet secretaries or military leaders.[23] This independence would remain one of the proudest characteristics of the analysts of the Central Intelligence Agency.

Like all experienced researchers, Donovan's professors in this Research and Analysis office began their work by reviewing the files of the existing intelligence offices in the army, navy, and even the State Department. Not surprisingly, they were "appalled" by the "haphazard and indiscriminate" official files but understood that secret information stolen by spies or reported by attachés is only a very small part of the information required by intelligence analysts. In fact, only 5 to

OSS Chief of Research and Analysis Professor William Langer's OSS identity card (Courtesy of the CIA).

10 percent of such raw information came from the "daring, courage, good luck, and tenacity" of the intelligence collectors assembled by Donovan in his Secret intelligence organization, and that is probably still true today.[24]

Fortunately, R&A experts had perfected their analytic and writing skills in long years of graduate study and academic life, and thus did not need the specialized military training given other OSS personnel. They did need data, however, and a worldwide network was set up to collect thousands of books, magazines, and newspapers, especially from within enemy countries. Because Donovan had a secret budget, he was able to hide the cost of buying all this material and shipping it back to Washington. In 1943, one overseas office alone was sending twenty thousand pages a week to R&A. Although the Germans tried to stop this flow of essentially "public" information, by the end of the war, OSS had accumulated some fifty thousand books and three hundred fifty thousand foreign magazines and newspapers.[25] Ironically, Donovan's insatiable researchers were often frustrated by their own American colleagues. Although Hillenkoetter's Pearl Harbor naval intelligence officers used decoded Japanese naval radio signals to warn of the attack on Midway Island and to plot Admiral Yamamoto's fatal flight plan, this priceless MAGIC information and the ULTRA intelligence produced from German Enigma code machines was not shared with R&A.[26] Similarly, while

Hillenkoetter's analysts learned much from interrogating Japanese prisoners of war, the OSS SI collectors withheld most of their secret reports, especially prisoner interrogations, from their analytic colleagues.[27]

Analysts complained bitterly to the chief of R&A, distinguished Harvard University historian William Langer. In one remarkable case, a "super-secret" report on the organization of the German army in Russia, supposedly received from General Charles de Gaulle's exile "Fighting French sources," turned out to have been an official Soviet press release published some time earlier in the *New York Times*.[28] The problem with spies like the French source is, of course, the need to trust them, especially if they claim to have unique access to very sensitive secrets. In most cases the SI intelligence collection officers were not experts on the information the spies were reporting, nor could they be expected to have deep knowledge about everything that OSS knew on any given subject. On the one hand, collectors, whether in OSS/SI or the later CIA Directorate of Plans, did like to believe that their spies were giving them valuable information of critical importance to the war effort, and they liked to think that they themselves were good enough judges of character to recognize if their spies were lying to them.

Historians, on the other hand, know very well that much information and many "facts" are wrong—or at the very least incomplete—and that people frequently seek to deceive. They thus put great store in trying to find out exactly where every fact comes from and in recording exactly how to know whether something is true. They want to know exactly where a source learned his information and whether that source had been reliable in the past. They are also accustomed to building great libraries and files—organized so that information can be quickly retrieved—and their goal, in the words of leading OSS and CIA analyst and Yale University history professor Sherman Kent, is "To know everything."

In the case of the Fighting French information, R&A carefully watched Soviet press releases about German forces and knew that this "super-secret" information had been published in American newspapers. This was by no means the only time that spies misled intelligence officers, and where possible, the OSS and later CIA emphasized what analysts call "original source material" like enemy documents such as the Japanese diaries, maps, and other materials captured on Guadalcanal and other war zones. In cases where spies were placed high in enemy governments, they were often ordered to either photograph the original documents themselves or, if possible, give their OSS managers original documents.

By the end of the war, R&A had grown to a staff of fifteen hundred in Washington, with a further four hundred fifty abroad in such field offices as London, Paris, and Stockholm. They had produced over twenty-five hundred reports and studies.[29] Most of R&A's experts were either historians or economists, but since

Professor Sherman Kent, leading OSS and CIA analyst (Courtesy of the CIA).

the focus of their studies was enemy countries in the midst of a global world war, they learned the urgency of working accurately and quickly to produce broad "area studies" needed by military commanders as well as political leaders. They also learned to focus on the very practical matter of using their training and skill to win the war. R&A economists, for example, carefully studied German transportation and industrial production to recommend where American and British strategic bombing could best be targeted to cripple the German war effort.[30] The R&A's first great challenge, which established its reputation for speed and accuracy, was the first Allied counterattack against the Germans: Operation TORCH in North Africa.

As recorded earlier by American diplomat Robert Murphy, Paris naval attaché Hillenkoetter had identified French North Africa as a promising area of Allied attack, and President Roosevelt had dispatched Murphy to develop a network of American offices and relationships with local French authorities. Murphy's vice-consuls, joined by more of Colonel Eddy's OSS officers, turned North Africa into the "most impressive" source of intelligence on the French military, but organizing effective resistance to the Germans proved much more difficult. As one vice-consul complained, "We worked . . . with what we had,"[31] and what they had were warring groups of conservative anti-republican royalists, Nazi sympathizers,

OSS Research and Analysis staff in London, 1944 (National Archives College Park, RG226-FPL, Box 1, R&A, 22 and 21).

supporters of arrogant General de Gaulle's Fighting French, and other assorted underground factions. All hated the British for "abandoning" France in 1940 and destroying the French fleet at Mers-el-Kébir on the coast of Algeria, and all of them feared their restive, Arab Moroccan, Algerian, and Tunisian colonial populations. And all of them begged Murphy and Eddy for funds and weapons.

Eddy, as a renowned Middle Eastern expert, thought an American invasion of North Africa would face only "token resistance," and Donovan budgeted $2 million for an armed underground uprising timed for the American landings. Two OSS officers even organized an irregular Arab army of ten thousand men, but the plan to arm colonial peoples alarmed the French and British and was rejected by Murphy. While OSS officers in North Africa were busy preparing to welcome General Eisenhower's army, Langer's R&A Europe-Africa analysts, led by expert in French history Sherman Kent, produced in fifty hours of around-the-clock work an "encyclopedic report" on Morocco, followed within two and a half weeks by comparable reports on Tunisia and Algeria. The military was impressed, and Donovan praised R&A for its "first victory."[32]

The Shadow Warriors of the OSS

Unfortunately, the first American invasion of the European war, on November 8, 1942, did not go nearly as smoothly. Underground groups in Morocco and

OSS Research and Analysis staff in London, 1944 (National Archives College Park, RG226-FPL, Box 1, R&A, 22 and 21).

Algiers, supported by the OSS, arrested Vichy officials and seized key locations, but the British Royal Navy had landed Eisenhower's troops in the wrong locations, and pro-Nazi authorities overwhelmed the underground forces before the Americans could reach them. Famous French general Henri Giraud, whom the Americans hoped would join them, refused to do so unless he, instead of Eisenhower, was given command of the TORCH army. Finally, after several days of fighting and the loss of hundreds of American and French lives, Hillenkoetter's old contact, Admiral François Darlan, now commander in chief of all French armed forces, ordered French forces to cease fire—but only after German troops invaded Vichy France. As Eisenhower's deputy, newly promoted Lieutenant General Mark Clark announced in great frustration, the "yellow bellied [French] sons of bitches" finally reached an agreement with American forces under which Darlan was to become chief of French North Africa.[33] The fighting allowed the Germans enough time to occupy Tunisia, and Darlan was assassinated by a young French royalist on Christmas Eve 1942.

Donovan's "calculatingly reckless" young SI and SO officers might have been chosen for their "ability to get along with other people,"[34] but in North Africa—and later in Italy, the Balkans, France, China, and Southeast Asia—they were thrown into political, ethnic, or religious situations that had festered for decades or, in some cases, hundreds of years. Most of the world had not enjoyed America's and Great Britain's representative democracy, and Germany, France, Italy, and Eastern Europe had been torn by decades of political and even physical battle among those who supported monarchs, those who wanted a communist workers' paradise, and a wide range of groups in the middle who wanted various types of democracy or liberty. Adolf Hitler had risen to power in Germany in 1933 out of exactly that sort of political turmoil.[35] Many OSS officers were refugees from these struggles, especially those European Jews who escaped anti-Semitism. Most other Americans were just as impatient with obscure kings or sectarian squabbles, and unsympathetic to the idea of protecting or restoring European empires. Trained for aggressive action, and often living with and growing to respect and admire their local underground allies, few OSS personnel worried about their hosts' political views as long as they were effective fighters, and few hesitated to express their own democratic sentiments, regardless of American diplomatic or military strategy—beyond the shared strategy of destroying Nazi Germany and imperial Japan. In Yugoslavia, for example, OSS officers often found communist partisan leaders hostile and obstructive, despite the tens of thousands of tons of supplies and munitions supplied to them. Finally, after unsuccessful attempts to deal with communist leader Josip Broz Tito's representatives, a frustrated OSS officer wrote "urgently suggest you . . . deal with the horse's mouth instead of wasting time at the other end."[36]

Another equally frustrated OSS officer, also speaking of the fighting between rival groups in Yugoslavia but making a universal point, wrote:

I personally do not feel I can go on . . . unless . . . every possible honest effort is being made to put an end to the civil strife. It is not nice to see arms dropped by . . . our airmen . . . be turned against men [who help us.] It is not pleasant to see our wounded lying side by side with the men who rescued . . . them—and to realize that the bullet holes . . . resulted from American ammunition fired from American rifles dropped from American aircraft flown by American pilots . . . . The issues in Yugoslavia . . . will have to be faced in many parts of the world. The Yugoslavians . . . have abandoned reason and resorted to force. Is this the shape of things to come? Are we all of us sacrificing to end this war only to have dozens of little wars spring up which may well merge into one gigantic conflict involving all mankind?[37]

Sadly, Yugoslavia would indeed prove to be one of the first pressure points of the long Cold War in which the new CIA became engaged, and after Tito's death, the country became one of the first great intelligence and military challenges of the post–Cold War world in the 1990s.

Their battle-hardened British mentors and allies often regarded the Americans as hopelessly naïve as well as pushy, and tried to control their activities. Like other Europeans, the British had long experience with secret activities and intrigues, and beyond that had been learning painful lessons for two years in the war before the OSS showed up. The British were happy enough to teach espionage, unconventional warfare, and sabotage and subversion skills in Special Operations Executive (SOE) training facilities, which Donovan then replicated and expanded in the United States near Washington, DC, and elsewhere, but they considered themselves the senior partners. Accordingly, the British tried to limit OSS activities and areas of operation, and even demanded that two-thirds of the mostly American support, supplies, and transport be committed to secret operations. Donovan and his officers, naturally aggressive, took a much broader view of America's areas of interest and sometimes suspected the British of violating hard-won agreements.[38] Only in October 1943, over the objections of the US Army in London, did OSS get JCS approval to conduct the kind of independent espionage that would be a hallmark of the CIA.[39] Even in the midst of great global war, individual prejudices and animosities were just as prevalent on the front lines as in the military commands or bureaucratic corridors of Washington or London.

France

Although the Allies were fighting a global war, Germany was the primary target and France the battleground recognized to best ease the pressure on the Soviet Union and lead directly to victory in Europe. As early as May 1943, Allied planners agreed to invade France, a decision approved by Roosevelt and Churchill in Quebec in August. By then the British had been operating spies in France for some time, as had the French themselves—and even the Poles.[40] American activities were constantly hindered by MI6 deputy Sir Claude Dansey, a "crusty old spirit" who repeatedly demonstrated "unnecessary combativeness and severe criticism of all things American."[41] He was especially protective of his own agents inside France and worried that American activities might expose or threaten his people. The French in exile in London were equally hostile, and while de Gaulle resented British actions dating to the fall of France and destruction of the French fleet, he also resented US support for Admiral Darlan and General Giraud in French North Africa. As later reported by William Casey, the British Special Operations Executive's goal was to

> encourage and enable . . . [the harassment of] the German war effort at every possible point by sabotage, subversion . . . raids, etc, and at the same

time build up secret forces . . . organized, armed, and trained to take their part only when the final assault began.[42]

There were many inside France willing to help, especially after Germany invaded the Soviet Union and French communists turned against the Nazi occupiers. Beyond that, Germany's plans to "draft" French workers for factory labor in Germany caused many thousands to flee to the mountains or forests—where they lived in hidden camps and were very receptive to SOE or OSS officers, who joined them with promises of training and weapons. Despite their retreat at Dunkirk in 1940, the British never really left France, and the SOE was very active. The first OSS officers arrived in June 1943, a year before the planned invasion across the English Channel, and by April 1944 French OSS agents, organized by eighty-five OSS personnel, were reporting to London by radio.

After the Operation OVERLORD D-day invasions on June 6, 1944, *Jedburgh* teams—made up of British, American, and French officers—parachuted into France to rally, arm, and train as many as three hundred thousand resistance fighters and to try to coordinate their activities with the invading Allied armies.[43] Among the brave American OSS officers who prepared the way for the Allied invasion was an extraordinary woman named Virginia Hall, whom the French

Male and female OSS *Jedburghs* preparing to parachute into occupied France, 1944 (National Archives College Park, RG226-FPL-T-117).

and Germans called "the woman who limps" because, like Colonel Eddy, she had an artificial leg.

From a wealthy Baltimore family, Hall studied in Europe and was fluent in French, German, and Italian. Athletic and adventurous, she served as an American embassy clerk in Warsaw, Vienna, and Turkey, where she lost a foot in a hunting accident. Because she was dismissed as a "crippled" woman, the State Department would not make her a diplomat, so when World War II broke out, she joined the French ambulance service until German victory in 1940. Recruited by SOE, she returned to Vichy France in August 1941 undercover as a neutral American reporter for the *New York Post*, setting up resistance networks just after Commander Hillenkoetter left the American embassy to return to sea duty. Beyond recruiting French agents and supplying them with training, money, and weapons, she helped escaped prisoners of war and downed airmen get out of France. After the American invasion of North Africa and the German occupation of Vichy France, she herself escaped by hiking across the rugged wintry Pyrenees mountains into Spain. The OSS sent her back to France in April 1944 to help prepare the French resistance for the great June OVERLORD invasion. The German *Gestapo* knew her from her SOE activities, so using false identity documents, she disguised herself as a weathered farm woman or cowherd so she could watch German troops and scout areas where the OSS could secretly drop supplies or weapons to her fighters.

In all, by moving constantly to avoid capture, she received fifteen airdrops, and in the month after Bastille Day, she transmitted thirty-seven reports back to London by secret radio. Originally helped and protected by thirty French fighters, she was joined by a joint OSS-SOE *Jedburgh* team after the Operation DRAGOON landings in southern France, and together they trained and equipped three French battalions that killed one hundred fifty German troops and captured five hundred prisoners. For her wartime heroism, she was made an honorary Member of the Order of the British Empire and, in September 1945, became the only civilian woman awarded a Distinguished Service Cross for World War II service.[44]

It's estimated that there were between one hundred thousand and three hundred fifty thousand resistance fighters inside France, but unfortunately, they were not always as effective as their numbers might suggest.[45] It was not only the British and Americans who were sometimes hostile to one another; the French were as well. As one Frenchman admitted, the resistance was plagued by a

nasty climate of constant and futile argument, frayed nerves, and hair-trigger tempers. [The OSS] declared with some vehemence that the only

CIA portrait of OSS officer Virginia Hall (Courtesy of Jeffrey W. Bass).

thing that interested them was that we fight the war . . . it made not the slightest difference to them whether we were partisans of one French general or the other.[46]

Beyond the petty infighting between factions, all of which demanded more and more weapons and supplies, the Allies worried that the rival resistance groups, especially the communists, were stockpiling weapons to fight their French rivals once the Germans were defeated.

Everyone who knew William Donovan considered him fearless, although his mild demeanor and pudgy appearance were sometimes deceptive. His senior representative in London was David Bruce, the multimillionaire son-in-law of steel magnate Andrew Mellon, who in later years was a distinguished American ambassador. Donovan originally asked Bruce to create the OSS Secret Intelligence organization, and when Bruce protested that he knew nothing of espionage, Donovan dismissed the protest by remarking, "Nobody else does."[47] In a meeting witnessed by Bruce with the American military intelligence chief in London, who made it obvious he didn't "trust General Donovan or his ideas," Donovan quietly responded, "Unless the general apologizes at once, I shall have to tear him to pieces physically and throw his remains through these windows."[48]

Clearly, even direct orders from Secretary of the Navy James Forrestal could not keep a man like Donovan from joining the D-day invasion, and he even wore his Medal of Honor ribbon as he and Bruce went ashore on the Normandy beaches. Belatedly realizing the foolhardiness of putting Roosevelt's chief of centralized intelligence at risk of capture as they came under German machine-gun fire—and discovering he had forgotten his OSS suicide pill—Donovan told Bruce: "David, we mustn't be captured, we know too much . . . . If we are about to be captured, I'll shoot you first. After all, I am your commanding officer."[49] The postwar OSS report called this kind of recklessness by senior officers who knew the ULTRA secret "clearly outrageous" and "simply not professional behavior."[50]

The Germans were initially paralyzed by the Normandy D-day landings, since the British had mounted a massive deception campaign to convince them that the "main attack," to be led by General George Patton's American army, would land farther north. As William Casey wrote, fifteen hundred people working on the deception program held down over two hundred fifty thousand German troops in twenty-two combat divisions. French saboteurs cut telephone and cable lines between Paris and Berlin, forcing the Germans to communicate by radio so that Allied code-breakers could listen in on the strategic debate between Field Marshal Hans von Kluge and Hitler about the best response to the Allied invasion.[51] On July 20, with the Battle of France still raging, senior German military officers tried to assassinate Hitler. Von Kluge, associated with these anti-Hitler officers, was recalled to Germany and committed suicide on August 17, two days after American troops landed in southern France in Operation DRAGOON, and as the Allies were nearing Paris.

David Bruce stayed with or ahead of American forces as they advanced toward Paris. Indeed, the American and British advance was often so rapid that the OSS and SOE struggled to put enough *Jedburgh* teams in front of them to rally French resistance and collect intelligence on the retreating German forces. In mid-August the Red underground of twenty-five thousand armed men rose up against the German occupation troops in the city, but de Gaulle's generals delayed dropping arms to the communists. At that time Bruce was twenty miles ahead of General Patton's army and noted in his diary: "It is maddening to be only thirty miles from Paris." Bruce and his new OSS officer Ernest Hemingway got a rude reception by French General Philippe Leclerc, commanding the Free French division chosen to have the honor of liberating Paris. As Hemingway recalled, Leclerc greeted them with an expression that the famous writer translated as "buzz off, you unspeakables."[52]

The American OSS officers were nonetheless welcomed by Parisians "almost hysterical with joy." On August 25, 1944, after surveying the last fighting from the top of the Arch of Triumph, Bruce and Hemingway toasted the liberation of Paris with martinis at the Ritz hotel. Bruce moved his OSS headquarters from London to Paris for the final push toward Germany. Speaking of the French agents and resistance fighters with whom they worked, fought, and sometimes died, one OSS officer said, "These are the kind of people worth respecting and the hell with the ones who were busy denouncing each other . . . to get political power."[53] Casey agreed, concluding that France liberated itself: "[Outside the area of the Normandy invasion] the huge area south of the Loire and west of the Rhone, as well as Paris, were liberated entirely by the [French] people and the FFI [French Forces of the Interior]."[54] Aside from Casey himself, another future director of the CIA, William Colby, led a *Jedburgh* team reporting on and harassing the German retreat.

Allen Dulles and the Penetration of Germany

The American invasion of southern France in August 1944 offered Allen Dulles, the OSS representative in Switzerland, his first opportunity to leave that small, neutral country—totally surrounded by Axis armies—since he had quietly ridden a train from Vichy France just a few days after Eisenhower's American troops landed in French North Africa in November 1942. The grandson and nephew of secretaries of state, Dulles had been a junior diplomat in Switzerland during World War I and later served at the Versailles Peace Conference and the American embassy in Berlin. Like Donovan, Dulles had become a prosperous New York lawyer. He toured Europe in 1933 as the Nazis and Italian Fascists were consolidating their power, even meeting and interviewing Hitler.[55] Having known Donovan while he was assistant attorney general, Dulles had, in January 1942, been offered the job of opening the Coordinator of Information's New York City office, where he worked on research and operations against Germany. Offered the position as David Bruce's OSS deputy in London, Dulles modestly but slyly asked for a "less glamorous post"—where he would be his own man, away from huge bureaucracies and Allied intrigues—and was given Bern.[56] In fact, as Dulles knew from his World War I experience—and as the OSS war report stated—"in both World Wars, Switzerland was the main Allied listening post for . . . European enemy and enemy-occupied countries."[57]

Allen Dulles's OSS identity badge (Courtesy of the CIA).

Over the next years he approached every American citizen living in Switzerland, most of whom agreed to help collect information on Germany and introduce him to the many enemy officials who visited Switzerland, as well as to the wide variety of anti-Nazi émigrés living in the small, neutral Alpine country. Dulles used the unconventional but very effective approach of calling himself President Roosevelt's special representative for Europe and working out of his apartment rather than the American embassy, so visitors could meet with him unnoticed. Soon anti-Nazi officers of Admiral Wilhelm Canaris's military intelligence organization, the *Abwehr*, approached him with the message that they hoped to overthrow Hitler and make a separate anti-Soviet peace with the United States and Great Britain. Heinrich Himmler—who, as head of Nazi security forces, including the SS and *Gestapo*, was Canaris's bitter rival—also began making overtures to the OSS after the German defeat by the Russians at Stalingrad in February 1943. Similar German messages also went to another "special Roosevelt representative" in Stockholm, OSS officer Abram Hewitt, but both American and British senior officials rejected these anti-Hitler, anti-Soviet overtures out of worry that their suspicious and paranoid Soviet ally, Joseph Stalin, would discover these discussions and think the Western Allies were double-crossing him.[58] Despite early assassination attempts in March 1943, and the spectacular bombing of his headquarters in July 1944, Hitler survived and ordered the killing of thousands of opponents, including Admiral Canaris. Himmler never dared to abandon him until the Russians entered Berlin, at which point he fled westward until captured by the British army.

Dulles also received a number of volunteers, including Nazi foreign ministry official Fritz Kolbe, known as "Wood," who was allowed to visit Bern periodically as part of his official duties.[59] Kolbe gave the OSS some sixteen hundred documents, primarily messages from German military attachés in some twenty countries. Anti-American British MI6 deputy Sir Claude Dansey doubted the authenticity of these stolen documents, but their accuracy was confirmed by ULTRA *Abwehr* intercepts.[60] As the OSS discovered after receiving supposedly supersecret Russian information—which the Free French had gotten from Soviet press releases and the *New York Times*—it is always prudent to confirm spy information from other sources. It is also wise to get secret information using the least risky method, and in this case the ULTRA material would have saved Kolbe from the very real danger of stealing German foreign ministry telegrams and smuggling them to Dulles in Switzerland, if Dulles or OSS R&A had known about ULTRA.

Ironically enough, the OSS office most intimately aware of ULTRA was X-2, the counterintelligence branch charged with catching foreign spies and protecting American secrets. In one of the great successes of military and intelligence history, at the beginning of the war in Europe, the British Security Service had captured the German spy network in England and had begun using captured German radio operators to send false and misleading reports to Berlin. Because this deception was managed by the so-called Twenty (XX) Committee, led by John Masterman, the entire process became known as the Double-Cross System.[61] Much of the information used to identify enemy spies—and confirm that the British deception was working and that the Germans believed the false reports from their spies inside England—came from ULTRA. Indeed, as one historian wrote, "The principal by-product of ULTRA was counter-intelligence."[62] Once the British shared both the Double-Cross success and the ULTRA secret with their American allies, it was decided that OSS/X-2 counterintelligence officers would employ decoded German messages to identify and capture German spies throughout Europe, and that special X-2 officers serving with American military commands would be responsible for safeguarding ULTRA and delivering this critical intelligence to army commanders. Only after the formation of the CIA would intelligence analysts and managers have routine access to such valuable communications intelligence, known as COMINT.

In neutral or occupied countries, the Allies were able to identify and work with local sympathizers, but both the OSS and British service saw the penetration of Germany "as an exceedingly difficult task, with a high casualty rate . . . expected." In fact, Germany had become so disorganized in the months before surrender— with hundreds of thousands of foreign workers and eastern *Volksdeutsche* ethnic German refugees fleeing from the advancing Soviet armies—that the spies had a "surprisingly low" casualty rate.[63] In the last nine months of the European war, thirty-four teams were safely parachuted into Germany, with seven using a re-markable new secret communication system called Joan-Eleanor (J-E), named after the wives of the inventors. Most OSS operators, including Virginia Hall, relied on bulky radio sets in suitcases, which demanded the use of codes and were subject to German detection and location. In late 1944, however, a two-part J-E high-frequency radio was invented. It was made up of a small, lightweight handset on which teams on the ground could talk directly to their managers in a specially equipped small British *Mosquito* airplane thirty thousand feet overhead, without being noticed by German security forces.[64]

In the final weeks of the war in Europe, the OSS had already begun planning for the occupation of Germany. Research & Analysis scholars were drawing up handbooks for the anticipated future Allied military government, compiling lists of Nazis to be arrested and anti-Nazi Germans who could serve in the new dem-ocratic German government. Professor Kent thought that the idea of bringing senior Nazis to trial, as was later done in the Nuremberg War Crimes Trials, was a waste of time, and wrote in his journal that the Allies should "simply single out the several hundred Nazis about whom there could be no doubt as to guilt, beginning with Hitler, and summarily execute them."[65]

Many OSS agents with forged papers from Stanley Lovell's R&D branch, wearing authentic German clothing, were penetrating Germany, with some of them even operating in Berlin.[66] Nazi officials were still trying desperately to halt the Russian advance on Berlin and the Soviet domination of Eastern Europe by making a separate peace with the West. SS General Karl Wolff, who command-ed German army forces in northern Italy, undertook talks in Switzerland with Dulles to surrender his forces and prevent Yugoslav communist Josip Tito's Red partisans from capturing the northern Italian port city of Trieste.

The Wolff initiative caused great concern about Russian reaction. Eisenhow-er's chief of staff General Walter Bedell Smith rebuked the OSS European chief, and Roosevelt's military chief of staff, Admiral Leahy, summoned Donovan to the White House for an explanation of Dulles's actions.[67] Stalin bitterly accused the West of making a separate anti-Soviet peace, and on April 4, 1945, President Roosevelt wrote him a stern response: It would be one of the great tragedies of history, if, at the very moment of victory now within our grasp such distrust, such lack of faith should prejudice the entire undertaking after the colossal losses of life . . . and treasure involved.[68]

A week later Roosevelt had died, and Harry S. Truman was president. A month later, on May 8, 1945, the war in Europe ended.

At the end of the European war, Donovan rejected the suggestion that Dulles be made chief of OSS Europe on the grounds that he was a "poor administrator" but appointed him chief of OSS Germany, largely because in Bern his "exceedingly small staff . . . succeeded in producing the best OSS intelligence record of the war."[69] Many experienced officers were already being transferred from Europe to the war still raging in Asia, and Dulles was put in charge of denazification. Sterling Hayden, an OSS officer who earned a Silver Star in Yugoslavia and went on to have a long and distinguished acting career, bitterly noted "the real anti-Nazis were dead, in exile, or in . . . Auschwitz, Buchenwald. Names we thought at the time . . . would teach us a lesson we'd never forget."[70]

The Soviets quickly returned Walter Ulbricht's German communists from their Russian exile and began establishing puppet governments in the territories occupied by the Red Army. As a disappointed OSS officer later recalled:

> Those were still days when we thought four-power cooperation might work, first in Germany and then . . . [at] the United Nations. Berlin is perhaps where that hope was first shattered . . . where we tried to make it work in a real situation.[71]

In the chaos of the collapse of Nazi Germany, the German military intelligence officer responsible for operations against Russia, Major General Reinhard Gehlen, hid his files and offered his services, and those of his experienced intelligence officers, to the United States.

This so-called Gehlen Organization, which later became the foundation of the Cold War German Federal Intelligence Service, continued its espionage operations in Soviet territory under the supervision of OSS officers Frank Wisner and Richard Helms, yet another future director of central intelligence.[72]

Major General Reinhard Gehlen, German Wehrmacht intelligence officer, from *Prologue* 39, no. 4 (Winter 2007) (National Archives College Park, RG238).

Asia

While most OSS activities in Europe were in support of large-scale military operations, in Asia the American military presence was relatively small, and OSS concentrated on rallying local populations for guerrilla and paramilitary operations.[73] The combat-hardened European veterans who joined their OSS colleagues already working in Asia found that the resistance groups fighting the Japanese were plagued with the same internal political strife that had complicated their operations in France, Italy, and the Balkans.[74] Beyond the rivalries among nationalists, communists, and, in China, even local warlords, however, the Americans found that almost all the local populations were deeply suspicious of the Western imperial powers of Great Britain, France, and even Holland. And those powers, especially the British and French, were equally suspicious of the OSS for its willingness to work—and in many cases sympathize—with local anti-colonial groups. When British Admiral Lord Louis Mountbatten, a great-grandson of Queen Victoria, Empress of India, was made Allied commander in chief of the

South East Asia Command (SEAC), Americans suspected he was focused on restoring the eastern empire, but he proved more supportive than General Douglas MacArthur, who barred the OSS from the Pacific theater, or army General Joseph "Vinegar Joe" Stillwell, who had the thankless job of dealing with the corrupt and incompetent Chinese Nationalist "Generalissimo" Chiang Kai-shek. Although officially Chiang's deputy, the sharp-tongued Stillwell called him a "peanut dictator," "an ignorant, arbitrary, stubborn man" who, with his "merry nest of gangsters," ruled China based on "fear and favor."[75]

Despite his justifiably sour disposition and his suspicion of unconventional guerrilla warfare, Stillwell did give OSS Detachment 101 a free hand to conduct anti-Japanese operations in Burma, telling them, "All I wanted to hear was 'Booms'" from the jungle. Lord Mountbatten was equally supportive, although some of his officers thought that "OSS would give undue encouragement to the aspirations to freedom of the subject peoples in Asia."[76] Det 101 Burma activities were considered "the most successful OSS guerrilla operations of the war," with

American General Joseph "Vinegar Joe" Stillwell with Chinese "Generalissimo" Chiang Kai-shek and Madame Chiang (National Archives College Park, "War and Conflict" album, photo 747).

just 500 Americans organizing, training, arming, and leading as many as 9,000 Kachin tribesmen, who attacked Japanese outposts, reported on enemy activities, and rescued downed aircrews.[77] By 1944 OSS was also working alongside Brigadier General Frank Merrill's famed Merrill's Marauders, the only American ground combat troops in the China-Burma-India theater at the time.[78] Although the OSS lost 15 Americans, Det 101 rescued 574 Allied fliers while killing at least 5,400 and possibly as many as 10,000 Japanese.[79]

A number of OSS officers had deep experience in Asia, with some having been Christian missionaries in China and feeling great sympathy for the impoverished long-suffering peasants and frustration at Chinese "disunity, the incompetence, the half-hearted . . . Chinese war effort."[80] As with General de Gaulle in France, Chiang's Nationalists too often seemed more concerned with saving their strength and stockpiling weapons to fight Mao Tse-tung's Red army than with driving out the Japanese. Ironically, because China was officially an ally, the OSS was never able to mount successful operations into Manchuria, Korea, and onward into Japan, in large measure because of relentless Chinese Nationalist opposition to OSS activities.[81] Neither could OSS operate in areas under the control of Mao's communists as they could in areas of Indochina occupied by Ho Chi Minh's Viet Minh. In summary, "OSS became accustomed to profound disappointment in its four years in China."[82] The final disappointment was that by order of President Harry Truman, OSS was terminated on October 1, 1945, just as Donovan was setting up observation stations in eight Chinese cities to conduct "long-range intelligence operations in China."[83] In Thailand, the OSS faced the same challenge, as one Thai explained:

> We have been free for over seven hundred years . . . . Why do you think we fear France, Great Britain, and China? Because they are all around us . . . uncomfortably close. We are for the United States because [you have] no territorial ambitions in Asia.[84]

Although the Japanese dominated the Thai government, that government "became in effect a resistance group working for OSS," cooperating so extensively that Thai police escorted OSS officers around Japanese-occupied Bangkok.[85] Unlike in Europe, where the OSS had to work with underground resistance groups, "there existed in [Thailand] what might best be described as a patriotic governmental conspiracy against the Japanese in which most of the key figures of the state were involved," including the chief of police, senior generals, the minister of foreign affairs, and the Regent.[86] Of course, as patriots, they saw their first responsibility to be to their own country rather than to the United States, a matter that later CIA officers would have to remember in working with "friendly liaison services" or allied governments around the world. And the most powerful incentive the OSS could offer was American support for postwar Thai independence against "suspected British designs."[87]

Next door, in French Indochina, the Japanese had left the French Vichy colonial government in place, although the OSS made contact with a frail and skinny revolutionary who called himself Ho Chi Minh and led the communist underground group known as the Viet Minh. Ho's fighters passed to the OSS intelligence about Japanese forces and helped rescue downed Allied pilots. The French, who wanted to restore their African and Asian empires, considered Ho "cunning, fearless, sly, clever, powerful, deceptive, ruthless—and deadly." His OSS contacts, in contrast, regarded him as "much more a nationalist than a communist," a "true patriot" who spoke American English after working as a waiter in New York and Boston, a man who loved to question them about the American Declaration of Independence. Ho "was convinced that America was for free, popular governments all over the world, that it opposed colonialism." Roosevelt seemed to encourage that view when just before his death he said, "[Indochina] should never be simply handed back to the French to be milked by their imperialists."[88]

After the destruction of Hiroshima and Nagasaki by atomic bombs in early August 1945, the Viet Minh rose across Vietnam and took control of Hanoi— although at the Potsdam Conference in July, Joseph Stalin, new president Harry Truman, and new British prime minister Clement Attlee agreed that the British should "liberate" southern Vietnam, while Chiang Kai-shek's Chinese Nationalists would do the same in Hanoi. An OSS team was the first to arrive in Saigon, followed shortly by British Indian Army General Douglas Gracey, who immediately imposed martial law and a curfew. In response to a general strike, Gracey armed the remaining French colonial troops, who brutally attacked Vietnamese civilians. In the ensuing Vietnamese retaliation, Gracey organized Japanese soldiers to fight alongside the British and French in a bloody "war of extermination." As a bitter observer noted, "The conclusion is inevitable that the French have learned almost everything under Hitler except compassion." Gracey ordered the OSS commander, a twenty-eight-year-old Chicagoan, Major A. Peter Dewey, out of the country, but he was killed at a Viet Minh roadblock by fighters who apparently mistook him for a Frenchman.[89] Dewey, who had parachuted into France in preparation for Operation DRAGOON, was the first American killed in what was to become a bitter thirty-year war between the Vietnamese and Western powers. In the north, the OSS escorted Ho Chi Minh to Hanoi, where he declared Vietnamese independence based on the model of the American Declaration of Independence and appealed for American support and investment. His

OSS escorts were met by another team of OSS and French officers, and as the senior French officer observed, "We seemed to the Americans incorrigibly obstinate in reviving a colonial past to which they were opposed." A Chinese army arrived in mid-September and looted Hanoi before returning north.[90] French General Philippe Leclerc, the liberator of Paris, replaced Gracey in October, and Ho's Viet Minh began the long underground war that finally drove the French out of Vietnam a decade later.

In China, World War II ended no less chaotically. General Stillwell had finally been replaced by General Albert Wedemeyer, after numerous complaints from Chiang Kai-shek. Wedemeyer argued that US forces should not get drawn in with Chiang's Nationalists in a civil war against Mao's communists. Many pro-Japanese Chinese warlords joined the Nationalists, and the OSS found itself caught in the middle. On August 25, 1945, just a week before the formal Japanese surrender aboard the battleship *Missouri* in Tokyo Bay, OSS officer Captain John Birch was stopped by a group of teenage Red peasant soldiers. Birch was a fundamentalist Baptist missionary who had just joined the OSS in May after serving as an intelligence officer for General Claire Chennault's pro-Nationalist Fourteenth Air Force, successor to the famed Flying Tigers. According to one account, the furious Birch said: "I want to find out how [the communists] intend to treat Americans. I don't mind if they kill me, for if they do . . . the United States will use the atomic bomb to stop their banditry."[91] Birch was shot dead, and four years later Chiang's Nationalists were driven from the mainland as Mao proclaimed the People's Republic of China.

The Postwar Vision

Well before Germany and Japan were defeated, General Donovan and his staff were already thinking of a permanent postwar national intelligence organization, one based upon the lessons they had learned during the war. As early as August 1942, his deputy, Brigadier General John Magruder, said, "Only a joint national intelligence service can lay bare all the facts and factors upon which a sound national decision can be based."[92] According to the OSS War Report, they "never lost sight of the fact . . . that [the OSS] was . . . an experiment of vital significance which . . . should determine the peacetime intelligence structure for the United States."[93] Most important, from Donovan's perspective, was preserving the skills and methods that the OSS had developed in analysis, counterintelligence, and espionage. In July 1944 Research and Analysis chief Professor William Langer said there was no need [to set] up a new secret intelligence and counter-intelligence service . . . because . . . the OSS [is] such an intelligence agency . . . . In short, the solution to the problem in the post-hostilities period is not . . . in further experimentation . . . but rather in the proper development, expansion and full exploitation of the facilities already available.[94]

Donovan saw unconventional propaganda and military operations as primarily wartime functions to be shut down with the coming of victory. In late 1944 the OSS had almost 13,000 people, including some 4,500 women. In all, about 7,500 served overseas.[95] In what the War Report called "typical Donovan [humor]," he teased military commanders that if they couldn't spare 2,000 or 3,000 troops for some task, he "would send twenty or thirty men to do the job." Privately, calling himself a "prudent realist," he admitted it would probably require 50 or 60 OSS personnel.[96] Still, with fewer people than a single army division, Donovan had built a service with officers and bases covering most of the world, along with support and administrative staffs to fund, train, and supply worldwide intelligence and military operations. He had also accumulated a number of enemies.

Harry Truman, Sidney Souers, and the Next Steps

Truman the Missourian

I̤T WOULD BE HARD TO imagine two successive presidents more unlike each other in background, experience, and personality than Franklin Delano Roosevelt and Harry S. Truman. Where Roosevelt was a member of a large, distinguished, and aristocratic eastern family—with a first-rate education and experience as a World War I assistant secretary of the navy, as governor of New York, and as a man who had rallied and inspired his fellow citizens during the Great Depression and Great War—Truman was a little-known midwestern farmer and politician from humble Scots-Irish origins with no formal education beyond high school. Whereas Roosevelt was devious and delighted in misdirection, Truman was plainspoken and straightforward. As the *Kansas City Star* noted with some surprise after Truman was unexpectedly nominated to be Franklin Roosevelt's 1944 running mate in the thoroughly corrupt and chaotic Chicago Democratic National Convention, the junior senator from Missouri had an "unusual capacity for development."[1]

As a child growing up in far western Missouri, Harry Truman was polite, gregarious, cheerful, and "conspicuously studious," characteristics that marked him throughout his whole life. He loved history and thought that by studying great men of the past, he could better understand human nature. As he told biographer Merle Miller: "Those people had the same troubles as we have now . . . . The only thing new in the world is the history you don't know."[2] He was too nearsighted to be admitted to West Point and only passed a Missouri National Guard eye exam by secretly memorizing the eye chart. Always a hard and careful worker, he gave up a well-paying job as a bank clerk in Kansas City to return to the rural family farm to help his father work the land. The First World War gave him an opportunity to demonstrate his leadership skills as captain of a National Guard artillery battery of Jackson County, Kansas City, Irish Catholics. His men respected him for his "great friendliness" and "warmth and liking for people," and through brief but intense fighting in the September 1918 Meuse-Argonne offensive, which finally convinced Germany to sue for peace, he never lost a man in combat.[3] He returned to Jackson County with high hopes, but the postwar recession of 1921 caused his small clothing store to fail, leaving him in debt for years. One of his National Guard friends was the son of Thomas J. "TJ" Pendergast, the powerful boss of the Kansas City Democratic Organization, and as Truman's store was failing, TJ offered him the support of the Kansas City Machine to become a Jackson County commissioner. Truman was enthusiastically supported by his former troops and proved hardworking, efficient, and honest. Despite that last trait, TJ helped him become chief administrator (called chief judge) of Jackson County in 1927, making him responsible for a larger population than some governors. Kansas City was a wide-open town, with much gambling, bootlegging, and prostitution, as well as government corruption and favoritism, but Truman's insistence on only hiring honest contractors who delivered high-quality work, rather than Pendergast's corrupt friends, caused TJ to call him "the contrariest cuss in Missouri."[4]

Pendergast would not support him for governor, nor for Congress, but in May 1934 encouraged Truman to run for senator, which he did as a dedicated Roosevelt New Dealer. In his campaign speeches he complained that 90 percent of the country's wealth lay in the hands of the richest 4 percent of the population, while millions were suffering. Prosperous Saint Louis businessman Sidney W. Souers—who went on to wartime service as a naval intelligence officer, ended the war as deputy chief of naval intelligence, and became Truman's first director of central intelligence and fast friend—was "appalled" at Truman's candidacy. As he recalled years later, "I would not hire that man in my business for more than $250 a month."[5] Thanks to huge vote majorities in Kansas City and Jackson County, Truman was elected to the US Senate, though many in Missouri and Washington sneeringly called him the "senator from Pendergast." In his first term, he began impressing his skeptical Senate colleagues as a quiet, conscientious hard worker through his investigation of railroad freight charges, bankruptcies, and reorganizations, and he was deeply moved when influential Republican Michigan senator Arthur Vandenberg made a point of being friendly to him. The railroad investigation confirmed his deep hostility to "high hats and privilege," as he saw the "wild greed" of New York lawyers, bankers, and Wall Street financiers profiting from the collapse of the railroad companies during the Great Depression. In a passionate floor speech he joked that Missouri outlaw Jesse James had to get up early and risk his life to steal $3,000 from the Rock Island Railroad, while modern financiers were easily stealing $70 million from the same railroad. "Senators can see what 'pikers' Mr. James and his crowd were alongside of some real artists."[6]

In 1939 TJ Pendergast confessed to tax evasion, and Roosevelt refused to endorse Truman for a second senate term. Still, in a tough race against popular reform governor and famed nurseryman Lloyd Stark in 1940, Truman again barely won, this time thanks to his popularity among blacks, farm whites, and city dwellers in Kansas City and Saint Louis. By now, world war had again broken out in Asia and Europe, and Truman, a strong supporter of military preparedness and a colonel in the Missouri National Guard, asked US army chief of staff General George C. Marshall to let him re-enlist. The army had turned down William Donovan's request for active duty, and Marshall told Truman he was too old and was more valuable in the Senate. Exactly how valuable he could be quickly became apparent when he took off on a personal driving tour of new army bases and defense contractors' factories to inspect the vast multibillion-dollar buildup that Congress had approved. He found so much waste and corruption by both labor unions and corporations that, in 1941, he was made chairman of a new special Senate Committee to Investigate the National Defense Program, called the Truman Committee. By now, even before the United States entered the war, the defense budget had ballooned to $13 billion, with another $7 billion allocated for lend-lease support to Great Britain and later Russia. Truman, as a careful student of history, was determined not to repeat the congressional meddling with military strategy that had plagued President Abraham Lincoln during the Civil War, and he was also determined to avoid political posturing or partisanship. His investigations and hearings would be polite and businesslike, and his annual reports would reflect the unanimous views of both Democratic and Republican senators. When asked how such remarkable consensus was possible, one Republican senator said, "It was not hard to get men to agree when the facts were known."[7] The committee focused on waste, corruption, and inefficiency in war production, and as longtime Florida congressman Claude Pepper said, "The man from Missouri had dared to say 'show me' to the powerful military-industrial complex, and he caught many people in the act." The one thing the committee could not uncover, despite repeated efforts, was the $2 billion secret known as the Manhattan Project. Only three congressmen, including Speaker Samuel Rayburn of Texas, were told that secret, and then only in February 1944, more than a year before Truman learned of it. Noted historian David McCullough called the committee a "masterstroke," one that saved the country an "enormous and unprecedented" amount, running into billions of dollars.[8] Truman was no longer seen as the puppet of a corrupt big-city boss but as a senator widely respected for his good cheer, honesty, integrity, and industry.

He was also known for his plain speaking. After Hitler attacked his former ally Joseph Stalin in June 1941, Truman bluntly said, "If we see Germany is winning we ought to help Russia and if Russia is winning we ought to help Germany, and that way kill as many as possible, although I don't want to see Hitler victorious."[9] Two years later in Chicago, he urged a safe haven for European Jews then being exterminated by "Nazi butchers," calling the Holocaust an American problem, rather than a Jewish problem, that must be faced "squarely and honorably." Beyond that, he launched a speaking tour on behalf of the United Nations Foundation, saying that the United States "could not possibly avoid the assumption of world leadership after this war."[10]

Truman the Global President

In 1944, through no fault of his own, and against his loud protestations, Truman was thrust into the highest levels of American leadership. Many in Washington feared that the strain on Roosevelt's health was so profound, and his physical decline so plain, that even if he did win a fourth term as president, he would not live through it. The man chosen as vice president was thus of critical importance. Roosevelt's current vice president, Henry Wallace, was unpopular in the South because of his liberal racial views, and South Carolina Senator James "Jimmy" Byrnes, a former Supreme Court justice who opposed integration, was equally suspect among liberals. Typically, Roosevelt refused to commit to either man, and indeed he encouraged both, even as his advisers were coming to the conclusion that, with his fine Senate record and his solid midwestern roots, Harry Truman was the one possible candidate with no major liabilities. The Democratic convention met in Chicago in July 1944 as American and Allied troops were fighting their way off Normandy beaches, German V-1 cruise missiles were falling on London, and fifty thousand Japanese troops and civilians were dying on Saipan island as American soldiers and marines captured that critical base from which to launch B-29 bombing attacks on the Japanese home islands. After much double-dealing and backroom plotting, Harry S. Truman of Independence, Missouri, was named as Franklin Roosevelt's running mate.[11]

The two men barely knew each other, and when they met for lunch in front of reporters and press photographers at the White House on August 18, 1944, the vigorous sixty-year-old Truman was shocked to see the frailty of the sixty-two-year-old president. Roosevelt said of Truman, "He doesn't know much about foreign affairs, but he's learning fast,"[12] but made absolutely no effort to enlighten him. Truman was told nothing about the February 1945 Summit in Yalta, at which Roosevelt, Winston Churchill, and Joseph Stalin supposedly resolved the

New vice presidential nominee Senator Harry S. Truman meeting President Franklin Roosevelt for lunch at the White House, August 18, 1944 (Office of War Information, Harry S. Truman Presidential Library, 66-2610).

framework for postwar Europe, although he very conscientiously read everything he could about the decisions made there. In essence, Truman saw his primary role as presiding over the Senate and acting as liaison between Congress and the White House. As popular as he was on the Hill, and as much as he enjoyed drinking, playing cards, and telling jokes with his congressional friends, it was an undemanding few months that scarcely prepared Truman for the job he would soon have to undertake.

On April 12, 1945, Truman was as shocked as anyone to find himself suddenly president of the United States. As he told reporters, "I've got the most terribly responsible job a man ever had."[13] In Berlin, Hitler rejoiced and declared that Germany would triumph even as the Red Army, the strongest military force in Europe, neared his ruined capital city. In Marburg in western Germany, fellow Missourian General Omar Bradley was with Supreme Allied Commander General Dwight Eisenhower and General George Patton when they learned that Harry Truman was now commander in chief. As Bradley, whom Truman would later appoint as chairman of the new statutory Joint Chiefs of Staff (JCS), admitted in his memoirs, "From a distance Truman did not appear at all qualified to fill Roosevelt's large shoes."[14]

Fleet Admiral William Leahy, who had been Roosevelt's chief of staff to the commander in chief and chairman of the Joint Chiefs—and would continue those high positions under Truman—worried "one cannot yet see how the complicated critical business of the war and the peace can be carried forward by a new president who is completely inexperienced in international affairs."[15] Those who knew him best were more confident. Speaker Rayburn predicted: "Truman will not make a great, flashy president like Roosevelt, but by God, he'll make a good President, a sound President. He's got the stuff in him." A Missouri historian later described Truman as a "highly experienced, methodical politician . . . endowed with an unpretentious but strong character, a clear and retentive mind, an independent spirit . . . common sense and self-reliance, and a formidable capacity for indignation and anger."[16]

He would need all these qualities as he suddenly began learning the terrible challenges facing him. His military commanders were predicting that the war

President Truman with Supreme Allied Commander Dwight Eisenhower and General Omar Bradley in Germany, July 1945 (Harry S. Truman Presidential Library, Box 53, 2000-3).

against Japan might drag on for another eighteen months, and General Marshall thought the invasion of Japan would cost a quarter-million American dead and as many wounded. The British were staggering under the terrible cost of a war they had been fighting for almost six years. Europe and Asia lay in ruins, with tens of millions dead and many more displaced, homeless, and hungry. A week earlier, American ambassador to Moscow Averell Harriman had reported: "We now have ample proof that the Soviets view all matters from . . . their own selfish interests . . . . We must clearly recognize that the Soviet program is the establishment of totalitarianism, ending personal liberty and democracy."[17] He called the Russian advance "a barbarian invasion" of Europe. The State Department concluded that the Soviets were breaking the commitments they had made to Churchill and Roosevelt and taking a hard line since their armies had already conquered all of Eastern Europe and were approaching Berlin. On April 2, 1945, an OSS analysis concluded, "Russia will emerge from [the war] as by far the strongest nation in Europe and Asia—strong enough if the US should stand aside to dominate Europe . . . . If Russia should succeed [in her expansionist policy] she would become a menace more formidable to the United States than any yet known."[18] Churchill, hated by Joseph Stalin because of the prime minister's fierce anti-communism, added his warnings about Soviet expansionism to those from the State Department and OSS.

Still, Truman, new as he was, had a number of advantages. He was commander in chief of sixteen million men and women serving all over the world and led by such brilliant officers as Chester Nimitz, George Marshall, and Dwight Eisenhower. He commanded the most powerful navy and air force the world had ever known, supported by the most innovative, wealthy, and efficient industrial economy in history. He had loyal and selfless advisers like Leahy and Marshall and a united country that, for all its sacrifices, had been spared the terrible destruction of Europe and Asia. But perhaps most promising and daunting, he had in his power the product of the $2 billion mystery that had frustrated his Senate investigative committee. In late April, Secretary of War Stimson and General Leslie Groves briefed him on the Manhattan Project, although Admiral Leahy, speaking "as an expert on explosives," doubted the atomic bomb would work.[19] Secretary of War Stimson, on the other hand, worried that it might mean "the doom of civilization." Within days, Russian and American troops met along the Elbe River in central Germany, Hitler committed suicide on April 30, and Berlin fell to the Russian army. May 8, 1945, marked the official end of the war in Europe.

At about the time the European war was ending, with the total destruction of the totalitarian Nazi police state, Truman was approached by FBI director J. Edgar Hoover with the offer of wiretap transcripts on leading Washington political figures. Roosevelt, with his love of gossip and intrigue, had told Hoover in 1936 to gather what he called political information. The scope of the FBI's effort can be seen in the Roosevelt Presidential Library in Hyde Park, New York, where visitors can view samples of the three-thousand-page file that the FBI compiled on the president's outspoken and active wife, Eleanor Roosevelt. Truman immediately and indignantly ordered Hoover to stop the wiretaps, telling the furious director that if he needed anything from the FBI, he would convey his request through the attorney general. In a May 12, 1945, memo, Truman wrote, "We want no *Gestapo* or secret police. FBI is tending in that direction. They are dabbling in sex-life scandals and plain blackmail . . . . This must stop."[20]

Truman's most controversial early decision was how to end the Pacific war against Japan, and whether to employ the atomic bomb, which had not yet been tested and even experts feared might either fizzle completely or destroy the entire world.[21] The Joint Chiefs had directed Pacific commanders General Douglas MacArthur and Admiral Nimitz to plan for a full-scale invasion of the Japanese home islands. Based on the bloody Battle of Okinawa and the initial landings at Iwo Jima, which had cost more casualties than the first day at Normandy, all involved expected the cost of an invasion of the home islands in both American and Japanese lives to be shockingly high.[22] American MAGIC intercepts showed that the Japanese were positioning their army and preparing the civilian population to fight to the death. Admiral Leahy again counseled caution, believing a naval blockade would starve the Japanese into surrender, and that it was unnecessary to invite the Soviet Union into the war. To Truman, the issues were: saving both American and Japanese lives by using the atomic bomb, assuming it would work to shock the fanatic Japanese leaders into surrender, and persuading Stalin to join the war against Japan, since an invasion might still prove necessary.

In some ways, the fate of Europe had already been settled by an enfeebled Roosevelt and an overconfident Churchill at Yalta in February 1945, well before new president Harry Truman faced Soviet dictator Joseph Stalin in the ruins of Berlin at the Potsdam summit in July. Although nobody yet knew it, America had already lost its staunchest foreign friend, because Churchill had already been voted out of office as prime minister by a war-weary British population. Truman said he was going to Berlin to meet "Mr. Russia" and "Mr. Great Britain," and studied hard on his way to the conference. Moscow ambassador Averell Harriman called him "astonishingly well-prepared." As had been his practice during his whole public life, Truman had a firm agenda he was determined to accomplish in a no-nonsense businesslike manner. He had already secured Soviet agreement to the creation of the United Nations (UN), but now he found Stalin surprisingly likable, if impossibly stubborn on European issues. As Truman's Russian translator and Soviet expert Charles "Chip" Bohlen said: "Stalin had perfected a talent for disguise . . . . There were no signs of the harsh and brutal nature behind his mask."[23] On the other hand, Truman found Churchill flowery and overtalkative. Unlike Roosevelt, he was not impressed with the man. Clement Attlee—the leader of the British Labour Party who would replace Conservative Churchill

President Truman with Secretary of State James Byrnes and Chief of Staff to the Commander in Chief Fleet Admiral William Leahy viewing the ruins of Hitler's *Reichskanzlei* (chancellery), July 1945 (United States Army Signal Corps, Harry S. Truman Presidential Library, Box 53, 64-375).

as prime minister halfway through the conference—was silent and played no significant role. To Truman's delight, Stalin quickly agreed to join the war against Japan but proved unbending on Polish boundaries or free elections. Truman was disappointed, but Leahy had considered Soviet domination of Poland, and indeed all of Eastern Europe, a *fait accompli* since Yalta.

Midway through the conference, Truman received confirmation of the successful A-bomb test on July 16, 1945, at Alamogordo, New Mexico, and five days later Secretary of War Stimson came to Truman's villa and read him and new Secretary of State Jimmy Byrnes the full account of the test results. On July 24 Truman, Churchill, and their combined military chiefs of staff again met at Truman's villa to discuss the implications of using the bomb in the war with Japan. To the Americans' surprise, Stalin seemed uninterested and incurious when Truman mentioned the bomb to him. For one thing, Stalin had probably already read transcripts of the Stimson report and deliberations with Churchill,

President Harry Truman with Soviet Premier Joseph Stalin and British Prime Minister Winston Churchill at Potsdam, Germany, May 1945. Fleet Admiral Leahy is in the background between Stalin and Truman (United States Navy, Harry S. Truman Presidential Library, Box 53, 64-377).

for without doubt, the Russians had bugged Truman's Potsdam villa as thoroughly as they eavesdropped upon Roosevelt in both Tehran in 1943 and Yalta in early 1945.[24] Much more seriously, Russian spies had penetrated both the British and the American atomic weapons programs almost from the beginning. By the time of the Alamogordo test, spies—many of them idealistic, committed communists—had given the Russians so much detail that the first Russian bomb in 1949 was based on the American design compromised by Klaus Fuchs.[25] Even before the end of World War II, the US Army Signals Security Agency had begun trying to break the supposedly unbreakable Soviet spy codes, and by 1948 the code-breakers were having dramatic success in revealing spies both in the Manhattan Project and within the wartime OSS. However, this code-breaking VENONA success was so secret that it could not be revealed during espionage trials, and even today many people incorrectly believe that such spies as Ethel and Julius Rosenberg were innocent victims of paranoid anti-communist McCarthyism.[26]

The US Army Air Force dropped two atomic bombs on Japan in early August, the results of which proved even more destructive than the relentless carpet-bombing the American and British air forces had inflicted on Germany and Japan in all the years of the war. General MacArthur received the Japanese surrender on the deck of Harry Truman's favorite battleship, *Missouri*, in Tokyo Bay on September 2, 1945, at which point Truman and his fellow Americans could perhaps be forgiven for thinking that the world would soon return to normal.

The Central Intelligence Agency and the Beginning of the Cold War

Not everybody felt so optimistic, however. Even before the war ended, Harry Truman appointed fellow Missourian General Omar Bradley to head the Veterans Administration. Bradley considered the assignment a huge challenge, and he expressed great anxiety about bringing home fifteen million veterans and ending the booming wartime industrial production. He feared "economic chaos: rampant, uncontrollable inflation, crippling unemployment . . . . Not many had faith that Harry Truman could safely steer the country through these turbulent economic waters."[27] Beyond simply demobilizing the great armies and re-absorbing the immense number of troops and sailors into peacetime American life, Truman faced the challenge of dismantling the giant military and governmental structure that had arisen to fight a global war. Even William Donovan recognized that the OSS would not survive in its wartime state, but as an optimist, he had hoped that his charm and the force of his logic could win over the new president. He and his men had already been pressing their case with Roosevelt, and Donovan had even given the president a proposal for an independent intelligence authority under presidential supervision. Roosevelt gave the "Donovan Plan" to his military chief of staff Admiral Leahy, who referred it to the Joint Chiefs. Saint Louis lawyer Clark Clifford, later President Truman's White House counsel, said the plan "enraged" the State, War, and Navy Departments. Clifford believed FBI director J. Edgar Hoover leaked the plan to the fiercely anti-Roosevelt *Chicago Tribune*.[28] In February 1945 hostile newspaper stories by Walter Trohan appeared, claiming Donovan wanted a "super *Gestapo* agency." In response, Roosevelt told Donovan to "shove the whole thing under the rug as long as the shock waves reverberate." Donovan blamed the Joint Chiefs or Hoover for the distorted leaks, but Trohan himself claimed that Roosevelt's press secretary had given him the OSS plan. As a historian of the early CIA put it, Roosevelt might have grown "weary and disenchanted with the flamboyant ambitious Donovan."[29]

Weeks after Roosevelt's death, powerful newspaper columnist Drew Pearson wrote:

> General "Wild Bill" Donovan of the Office of Strategic Services, sometimes called the "Cloak and Dagger Club" or "Oh so Social" will miss Roosevelt terribly . . . . As an old personal friend, Roosevelt gave him free rein, including grandiose plans for a postwar espionage service. Truman does not like peacetime espionage and will not be so lenient.[30]

Indeed, Donovan had actually appeared before the Senate Truman Committee in 1943 but used claims of "national security" and his legal skills to avoid answering their questions in full. Press reports suggested that Truman had vowed to investigate OSS abuses after the war. He certainly didn't like J. Edgar Hoover's scandal-mongering but appeared now also to associate Donovan's OSS with the *Gestapo*. The president's senior military adviser, Fleet Admiral Leahy, seemed to hold the same view, especially after rebuking the OSS for secret negotiations between the north Italian SS commander, General Karl Wolff, and Allen Dulles, which aggravated Stalin's paranoia. In a memo to Truman on May 16, 1945, Leahy called Donovan a "loose [cannon] on deck." Finally, in the words of one historian: "Truman simply did not like self-promoters."[31]

Accordingly, the new president left it to his budget director, Harold Smith, to "liquidate the war agencies and reconvert the government to peace." Truman told Smith he had his own ideas for a "broad intelligence service attached to the President's office," but in the meantime to dissolve the OSS. As noted British intelligence historian Christopher Andrew observed: "[He] was clearly confused about what he wanted. Truman's main priority was probably for a more orderly system for providing him with intelligence reports . . . but he remained anxious to avoid . . . anything that resembled his vague idea of a '*Gestapo*.'"[32] Truman said so himself years later: "I needed . . . a central organization that would bring all the various intelligence reporting we were getting . . . and there must have been a dozen of them, maybe more, bring them all into one organization so that the President would get one report on what was going on in various parts of the world."[33] Donovan was still trying to give him the same message, writing on August 25, 1945, "The formulation of national policy both in its political and military aspects is influenced and determined by knowledge (or ignorance) of the aims, capabilities, intentions, and policies of other nations."[34] However much Truman agreed with Donovan on that point, he did not want Donovan's OSS giving him that knowledge, and he appeared not to understand that intelligence could benefit from centralized and coordinated collection and analysis even more than from a centralized "coordinator of information" that simply compiled reports from rival intelligence agencies.

On October 1, 1945, therefore, OSS's 1,655 Research and Analysis staff,[35] including such brilliant men as William Langer and Sherman Kent, went to the Department of State, while the 9,000 espionage and counterintelligence personnel went to the army as a Strategic Services Unit (SSU) under General Magruder, who managed to maintain the OSS Eastern Europe, Balkans, and China networks[36] as part of his effort to preserve "the holy cause of central intelligence."[37]

Donovan was dismissed with a letter from Truman, which offered cold comfort: "Great additional reward for your efforts should lie in the knowledge that the peacetime intelligence services of the [US] are being erected on the foundation of the facilities and resources mobilized through the Office of Strategic Services during the war."[38] As his new naval aide Clark Clifford said, Truman "prematurely, abruptly, and unwisely" terminated the OSS, "persuaded by bitter critiques from army intelligence . . . inspired by jealousy."[39]

Within months, as the situations both domestically and abroad grew more chaotic, and the intelligence disorganization and duplication even worse, Truman again turned to Admiral Leahy to manage the problem. Leahy, however, had plenty of other crises demanding his attention. The Russians were tightening their grip on Eastern Europe. The deteriorating situation between Mao's Reds and Chiang Kai-shek's Nationalists caused Truman to dispatch retired General

George Marshall as his special envoy to China in November 1945. Marshall was replaced as army chief of staff by Supreme European Commander Dwight Eisenhower, and Ike's former chief of staff, Walter Bedell Smith, went to Moscow as ambassador. Pacific Fleet commander Chester Nimitz became Chief of Naval Operations.[40] Both Eisenhower and Nimitz agreed on the desirability of a National Intelligence Authority, but Secretary of State Jimmy Byrnes's new intelligence chief, army colonel Alfred McCormack, thought he should direct that authority.[41] Since OSS analytic experts had been given to the Department of State, and since the Foreign Service had traditionally prided itself on collecting foreign political and economic information—analyzing and managing foreign

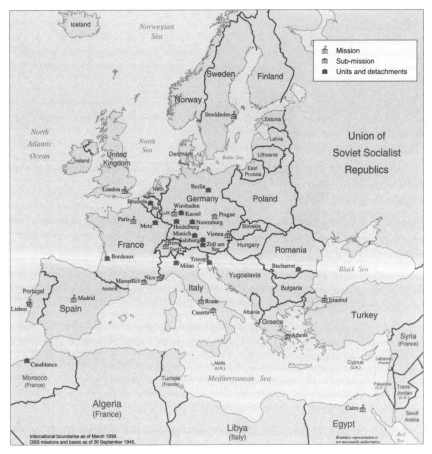

OSS field offices just before President Truman dissolved the wartime organization in September 1945 (Courtesy of the CIA).

relations and diplomacy, and acting as the president's primary international affairs adviser—this was not an unreasonable view. Indeed, in the years between the dissolution of the OSS and the creation of the CIA, most Washington maneuvering about intelligence management had more to do with who should direct the various departmental intelligence offices and less about Donovan's vision that intelligence professionals should be combined within a single organization—or Truman's desire for a single agency to produce his "newspaper." In the words of OSS analyst Sherman Kent, Colonel McCormack was a "hard-boiled and successful administrator," "unwilling [. . .] to back down in a fight." Longtime State officers feared "so strong, so tough and able a character on their turf," and he

OSS field offices just before President Truman dissolved the wartime organization in September 1945 (Courtesy of the CIA).

was soon replaced by the former chief of OSS, Research and Analysis's William Langer. Langer too soon fled back to Harvard's history department, and Kent recalled, "I don't suppose there had ever been or could ever be a sadder or more tormented period in my life."[42] And beyond all of that, it was evident to Leahy and many others that the American military structure, with its separate Army and Navy Departments and its powerful Army Air Force, required re-organization and consolidation into a unified Department of National Defense with an independent Air Force.

Accordingly, Leahy turned to others to deal with national intelligence. Chief of Naval Intelligence Admiral Thomas Inglis had told the brilliant and driven Secretary of the Navy James Forrestal that the new director of national intelligence must be a man of "mature judgement, of great tact, and yet considerable force of character, because he would be dealing with a number of conflicting personalities, a number of conflicting interests."[43] According to Inglis's new deputy, Missouri businessman Rear Admiral Sidney Souers, Forrestal wanted navy captain Hillenkoetter for the job, but Leahy and the chief of naval operations insisted on Souers because he was more familiar with military National Intelligence Authority proposals.[44]

In his recollections of his time as ambassador to Vichy France, Leahy had commented on his dismay at the nautical ignorance of his new "assistant naval attaché," OSS officer Thomas Cassady, and in many ways Rear Admiral Souers was an equally improbable naval officer. Born in Dayton, Ohio, in 1892, Souers graduated from Miami University, Ohio, where he lettered in track and basketball and captained the wrestling team.[45] He worked as a banker and business executive for grocery store chains and insurance companies in New Orleans, Memphis, and Saint Louis. Known for strengthening faltering companies, he was not impressed with Kansas City–machine politician and new senator Harry Truman. He did, however, have business dealings with New York financier James Forrestal, just a month older than himself, and each was impressed with the other. In the words of an intelligence historian, "Souers was a steady and sagacious man, skilled at getting people to work together."[46] In 1929 he was commissioned a navy reserve lieutenant commander and "senior intelligence officer" in Saint Louis, responsible for public relations, officer recruitment, and "investigating the development of the intelligence organization."[47] At the age of forty-eight, he gave up his wealthy corporate life, and went on active duty in July 1940, taking a pay cut from $30,000 to $3,000 a year.[48] In his words, "A lot of things were more important than money at that time." In February 1942 he was made district intelligence officer in Charleston, South Carolina, responsible for counterintelligence, prevention of sabotage in the port of Charleston, and interrogation of captured

German submarine personnel. During his time in Charleston, the first German submarine survivors of World War II captured by Americans were put in his charge when Coast Guard cutter *Icarus* sank the *U-352* on May 9, 1942, off the Carolina coast.[49] So early in the war, there was considerable confusion about how to deal with prisoners of war, and the thirty-three Germans were in the water for a half hour while the elderly lieutenant in command of *Icarus* sought instructions on whether to rescue them. This gave the tough and security-conscious U-boat commander, Lieutenant Hellmut Rathke, plenty of time to warn his crew not to reveal military secrets. Even after they were brought ashore, the "conspicuously arrogant" Rathke was kept with his crew and was thus able to exercise discipline over his sailors—four of whom had relatives in the United States.

Nonetheless, Souers was able to produce an impressively detailed *Post Mortem of Enemy Submarines* in which he expressed the hope that the document would be the first of many such reports of captured prisoners.[50] Beyond garnering details about the submarine and its crew, Souers also oversaw questioning about

Commander Sidney Souers (*right*) and US Navy and British Royal Navy officers with captured German marine prisoners, April 10, 1942 (United States Navy, Harry S. Truman Presidential Library, 96-1008).

a British commando raid on the French port of Saint-Nazaire in March 1942, which had destroyed its large naval dry dock. His conclusion was that "there is little doubt that these men honestly believe that the British commando raid . . . did comparatively little damage."[51] Indeed, the German submarine base and its armored U-boat pens were undamaged, and the British lost two-thirds of their raiders.

After a few months in Charleston, Souers transferred to San Juan, Puerto Rico, where he again served as district intelligence officer and staff intelligence officer to the naval commander of the Caribbean Sea Frontier. Years later Souers recalled that his business friend Forrestal, undersecretary and later secretary of the navy, had first offered him a navy financial administrative assignment, but Souers wanted active service. Finding himself "lonely and bored" in Puerto Rico, he turned to Forrestal to help him become deputy chief of ONI under Inglis, who opposed Donovan's plan for an independent "autocratic" director of central intelligence.[52] Inglis was honest enough to recognize that the jealous feuding between intelligence organizations was unhelpful. Referring to wartime tensions between OSS and army intelligence, the admiral noted, "You would have thought that one was the enemy, rather than the Germans and the Japanese."[53]

Souers, therefore—along with another improbable naval officer, White House counsel and Saint Louis lawyer Clark Clifford—drew up an Executive Order creating a National Intelligence Authority made up of military and foreign affairs senior officials to direct a new Central Intelligence Group (CIG), whose first task was to produce a national intelligence digest to answer Truman's repeated demand: "Where's my newspaper?"[54] The reluctant Souers agreed to serve as the first director of this CIG for six months before returning to his Saint Louis business interests, and Truman noted with great satisfaction: "I now began to receive a daily digest and summary of the information obtained abroad . . . . Here at last . . . a practical way had been found for keeping the President informed as to what was known, and what was going on." In his memoirs, Truman said, approvingly, that the CIA later gave his advisers consolidated estimates from all American intelligence organizations when policy required a presidential decision.[55] The new director of central intelligence, who had first met President Truman while drafting the Executive Order of January 22, 1946, was usually Truman's first visitor of the day.[56] Clifford called Souers a "quiet, undemonstrative man with good common sense," adding that "despite [his] disclaimers, Leahy, Forrestal, and I agreed that he would be ideal as the first Director of Central Intelligence."[57] As he had hoped, he did indeed soon turn intelligence leadership over to new directors, but Souers remained loyally at Truman's side as executive secretary of the new National Security Council (NSC), which replaced the National Intelligence Authority as Truman's national security and intelligence advisers, and he became one of the president's most devoted friends. Distinguished Harvard scholar Richard Neustadt, who served in the Truman White House, called Souers a "nonpartisan, neutral careerist" serving as key conciliator between departments and military services.[58]

Two days after authorizing the Central Intelligence Group, President Truman summoned his new director of central intelligence (DCI) and his senior military aide to a White House ceremony. From early adulthood, Truman had loved the brotherhood, ritual, traditions, and ceremony of the Masons, and had taken equally enthusiastically to the fellowship and rites of the United States Senate.[59] Perhaps deliberately parodying journalistic scold Drew Pearson's attack on Donovan and his "Cloak and Dagger" OSS, and certainly teasing the formidable and dignified Fleet Admiral Leahy, the president announced:

> By virtue of the authority vested in me as Top Dog, I require and charge that Front Admiral William D. Leahy and Rear Admiral Sidney N. Souers receive and accept . . . positions as Personal Snooper and Director of Centralized Snooping. In accepting these symbols of trust and confidence, I charge that each of you not only seek to better our foreign relations through more intense snooping but also keep me informed constantly of the movements and actions of the other, for without such coordination there can be no order and no . . . mutual trust.

He then presented them with black hats, cloaks, and wooden daggers, adding a fake mustache for Leahy.[60] A year and a half later "Senior Shellback" Leahy would exact his revenge when he accompanied the president and his family back from a conference in Rio aboard *Missouri*. Crossing the equator for the first time by sea, "pollywog" Truman was forced to bribe King Neptune with cigars for his use of a "despicable and unnatural" airplane to reach Rio, while daughter Margaret had to sing "Anchors Aweigh" with new junior officers.[61] During his presidency, Truman vacationed frequently at the "little White House" in Key West, Florida, and while Souers and other White House staff routinely wore gaudy Hawaiian shirts there, the dignified Leahy often wore his sober khaki naval uniform—even when fishing.

The first few months of 1946, in many ways, set the strategic tone for the decades to follow. At Truman's invitation, former British prime minister Winston Churchill journeyed to tiny Westminster College in the small central Missouri town of Fulton to deliver an eloquent appeal for Western nations to join together

Fleet Admiral Leahy, chief of staff to the commander in chief, fishing off Key West, November 22, 1946 (Album titled "The President's Vacation Trip to Key West, 17-23 November 1946," Harry S. Truman Presidential Library, 63-1373-65).

in the new United Nations, warning that "an Iron Curtain has descended" across the center of Europe.

In Moscow, intense diplomat George Kennan took advantage of the temporary absence of the American ambassador to send home his famous "Long Telegram" analyzing the Soviet Union and its global strategy and proposing that the United States "contain" the Soviet threat. And the navy dispatched its most famous battleship, *Missouri*—the Tokyo Bay "Surrender Ship" now under the command of Captain Hillenkoetter—to the Mediterranean to demonstrate the global reach of American military power to Turkey, Greece, and Italy, and to serve as a warning to communist guerrillas and political parties threatening the governments of those nations.[62]

Fleet Admiral Leahy and National Security Council Executive Secretary Sidney Souers at Little White House, Key West, November 21, 1951 (Album titled "Rear Admiral Robert Dennison," Harry S. Truman Presidential Library, 98-1826).

In late spring of 1946 President Truman offered his first proposals for a new national security structure. As Clark Clifford remembered, Truman quipped that "if the army and the navy had fought our enemies as hard as they fought each other, the war would have ended much earlier."[63] Clifford noted that "the struggle over the structure and mandate of the CIA was obscured in the public eye by the noisy battles over the unification of the services and the National Security Council . . . . Fierce disagreement . . . raged. . ."[64] By now Souers, who was trying to end his Washington service, had identified his successor as director of the Central Intelligence Group: Army Air Force Lieutenant General Hoyt Vandenberg. Clifford called the youthful and dashing Vandenberg "a man in a hurry . . . clearly marked as a star of the next generation."[65] Making him even more appealing was the fact that his uncle, Michigan Republican Senator Arthur Vandenberg, was a powerful member of the Senate Foreign Relations Committee who had made a dramatic conversion from being a traditional pre–World War II anti-Roosevelt isolationist to being a strong proponent of the bipartisan internationalist foreign

President Truman and former British Prime Minister Winston Churchill arrive in Jefferson City on their way to Westminster College in Fulton, Missouri, March 5, 1946 (Courtesy of the Missouri State Highway Patrol, Harry S. Truman Presidential Library, Box 26, 61-202-6).

policy being developed by Truman's administration. Vandenberg, who had his eye on becoming the first chief of staff of an independent Air Force, was reluctant to become DCI until the sharp-tongued Souers asked him "if he thought he would be made Chief of Staff just because he was handsome."[66]

Vandenberg replaced Souers as DCI on June 10, 1946, and Souers was relieved of active duty in July—the same month that Hillenkoetter returned to Paris for his third tour as naval attaché. Even after the American embassy in Vichy was closed, the Office of Naval Intelligence (ONI) took great interest in France, and even before the defeat of Nazi Germany, naval attachés were writing the same kinds of internal and international political reports they had done under Ambassadors Bullitt and Leahy. The OSS and Ho Chi Minh had been bitterly disappointed by France's determination to reclaim its Indochinese colony, and local populations in Algeria and the Levant (now Lebanon) also were restive. In a letter from Paris to his ONI colleague in Washington in April 1945, Captain D. D. Dupre reported driving to the former American embassy in Vichy to recover the attaché office equipment and furnishings abandoned in 1942.[67] He also tracked down a longtime French employee, Miss Louisiana Cornille, in her small village

US Air Force General Hoyt Vandenberg after his service as DCI
(Courtesy of the CIA).

several hours south of Paris and brought her back to work for him. "As you
know, she has had about 20 years in the Naval Attaché's office in Paris and is, is
of course, invaluable."[68]

Dupre's *Political Summaries* discussed French political parties, unrest in Algeria,
and de Gaulle's "aggressive" nationalism. He predicted

> once the war ceases to exert its unifying influence, de Gaulle will have the
> greatest difficulty retaining the confidence of the left parties. Many resis-
> tance leaders have come to believe that he no longer represents them . . . .
> They feel that in domestic policy his "drift to the right" has taken him off
> the middle ground where compromise is possible without the surrender of
> vital principles.[69]

Political disarray and internal rivalry were no surprise to the OSS, nor did they
come as a surprise to the senior American naval attaché returning to Paris in July

1946 for his third tour of duty, rejoining his friends, the Douglas MacArthur family. While Hillenkoetter had spent the war years in the Pacific, MacArthur spent almost two years in Nazi internment after the Germans occupied Vichy France in 1942. As MacArthur later recalled, OSS officer Thomas Cassady was also interned, although the unfortunate Cassady was briefly tortured by the Germans, who rightly suspected him of being an intelligence officer.[70] A decade earlier Hillenkoetter had been an obscure long-service naval officer with an unusual gift for languages; now he was an experienced intelligence officer and manager and the celebrated former commander of the world's most famous battleship. Newspaper journalists pointed out the great respect he enjoyed with former resistance fighters, many of whom were now active in the French government. Relations with the French navy were even closer, since many French sailors had served in the US Navy during the war and felt "genuine admiration and friendship for us."[71] In Hillenkoetter's semiannual report to ONI, covering almost the entire period of his service as attaché, he noted that his six officers were busy with inspections of ports, shipyards, war damage, and scuttled ships, and "constant liaison . . . with French naval officials, prominent French civilians, foreign attachés, US military officials, and prominent American business and professional men."[72] The report includes an extraordinary accounting of Hillenkoetter's social calendar, with official lunches, dinners, receptions, or ceremonies almost every day, leaving him only a single week for an inspection trip to Germany, Norway, and Denmark, and two days in Madrid.

He praised the close cooperation and intelligence sharing between his office and his US Army counterparts, and "the complete informality and even considerable friendship" with embassy diplomats. "The Ambassador [Jefferson Caffery] continues to manifest his complete confidence and satisfaction . . . and speaks with the most complete frankness." Cooperation with his British counterparts was equally close, both in terms of intelligence sharing and in coordinating collection and inspection trips: "The most complete confidence and friendliness exists." Not surprisingly—but very useful because of Soviet designs on the Dardanelles, Greece, and Turkey—"complete intimacy and frankness exists with the Turkish Attaché—mainly as a result of the present Naval Attaché having commanded the *Missouri* on her visit to Turkey last Spring."[73]

Hillenkoetter assured Washington that "particular attention will be given to the continuing delicate political situation in France and to the political position of the Communist Party . . . . It is expected that the next six months will bring important modifications . . . either bringing [the Party] to complete power or reducing its present vast influence."[74] Before his prediction could be played out, the new rear admiral found himself back in Washington leading the US government's secret covert action campaign to support anti-communist political parties in Western Europe, and the communists never did achieve complete power in France, Italy, Greece, or Turkey, despite their success under threat of Soviet military power in Eastern Europe. As it had been at the end of the 1930s, a decade later France was still an important intelligence-collection target, and the chief of naval intelligence praised the Paris office: "The quality and number of intelligence reports . . . have been outstanding."[75]

Hillenkoetter and his attaché colleagues did have one bitter complaint. While France had suffered major war damage, especially after the June 1944 Normandy invasion, Paris had been doubly spared. In 1940 American Ambassador Bullitt persuaded the advancing German Army to consider Paris an open city rather than inflicting on it the destruction visited on Warsaw and Rotterdam. In August 1944 the German military governor, General Dietrich von Choltitz, surrendered his garrison to the Free French rather than obey Hitler's order to level the city. Even at the end of a long and bitter war, Paris was a lovely city, while London—after six years of austerity, bomb shelters, and bombing and missile attacks—stood battered and grim. Given a choice, therefore, Paris was an irresistible destination for "casual visitors." In Hillenkoetter's words: "There is no let-up whatsoever in the innumerable calls for services of every sort having no connection whatsoever with our naval activities or intelligence . . . for people 'drifting in.' This is an old racket but greatly increased since the war."[76] Even such things as finding housing, transportation, and food required great effort, and acting as travel agent for self-important senior visitors, beyond the great number of official guests, was not high on Hillenkoetter's list of priorities.

Back in Washington, new DCI Vandenberg and his general counsel, Lawrence Houston, immediately agreed that, in the words of White House counsel Clark Clifford's colleague, George Elsey, "experience had shown that [the Central Intelligence Group] would be ineffective if it remained only a small planning staff [dependent on hostile rivals for both personnel and funding] and that it must now become a legally established, fairly sizable, operating agency." Houston, an OSS field officer in Cairo, had served as Brigadier General Magruder's general counsel at the army Strategic Services Unit, and when Souers became DCI in January 1946, Houston became his general counsel, a position he held for every director of the CIA until his retirement in 1973. A Missourian by birth, Houston was born on January 4, 1913, in Saint Louis, where his father was chancellor of Washington University.[77]

Truman also agreed but insisted that the new Defense reorganization come first.[78] The president continued to maintain that position even as Vandenberg became more and more frustrated and agitated.[79] In fighting to establish the superiority of his position as director over the other service agencies, Vandenberg did, however, create one of the most important missions of the later CIA: the production of National Intelligence Estimates combining the considered judgments of all US intelligence agencies.

Although handicapped by a severe shortage of skilled analysts—with most of the former OSS experts still stuck within the inhospitable State Department or back at universities—Vandenberg's analysts in his new Office of Research and Estimates managed to draft and coordinate some twenty Estimates, beginning with ORE I in July 1946, about worldwide Soviet capabilities and intentions.[80] Truman was the first president to appreciate that the most important mission of intelligence is to help the chief executive and his senior policy advisers understand foreign adversaries and threats, and that a centralized agency reporting directly to him was the best way to deliver impartial advice. There will always be plenty of advice coming out of the State Department, military services, and even Congress, but each entity has its own policy preferences, and ideally, a DCI, working only for the president, should be able to see beyond his own narrow agency interests. That was, at least, the goal of the men and women who followed William Langer and Sherman Kent back into Truman's new CIA several years later.

In 1945 the exhausted British voters had, as Truman discovered at Potsdam, swept heroic wartime leader Winston Churchill from power, and in November 1946 American voters gave the Republicans control of Congress. Demanding an end to wartime wage limits, union leader John L. Lewis threatened to shut down coal mines, which would cripple American industry, and DCI Vandenberg's uncle became Chairman of the Senate Foreign Relations Committee. Beyond turmoil at home, Truman had just received a consolidated report from diplomatic, intelligence, and military leaders about Soviet aggression, drafted by Clark Clifford, which the sobered president called "powerful stuff."[81] In the words of Missourian General Bradley, the Soviet Union was

> undeniably and unequivocally the main enemy of the United States and free men everywhere . . . . Stalin leered hungrily over the prostrate carcass of Western Europe, initiating intense political action programs designed to expand the growing communist blocs in the French and Italian assemblies . . . . He was backing Greek insurgents in open warfare against the . . . government.[82]

By early 1947 the secretaries and chiefs of staff of the army and navy, with Leahy as their chairman, had reached general agreement on a new defense and national security structure. In February, the impoverished British announced they could no longer militarily support Greece and Turkey, a region that the United States had always regarded as within Britain's sphere of interest because of the proximity of the Suez Canal. New Senate Foreign Relations Committee Chairman Arthur Vandenberg told Truman that before acting to take up the mantle the British had let fall, Congress needed to hear him urge support for these countries. He did so in an address to Congress on March 12, 1947, in which he stated, "I believe it must be the policy of the United States to support free peoples who are resisting attempted subjugation by armed minorities or by outside pressures." Some Republicans refused to stand to greet the president, but Clifford called it "the opening gun in a campaign to bring people to the realization that the war [wasn't] over by any means."[83] This Truman Doctrine of American support to countries threatened by communism was followed less than three months later by a speech given by new Secretary of State Marshall in which he stressed that it was imperative that the United States help rebuild the shattered Western European nations. The $10 billion Marshall Plan represented a full 16 percent of the entire US national budget.[84] The plan was drawn up by Marshall's undersecretary, Dean Acheson, with Clifford calling it Acheson's "crowning glory." "In a city filled with large egos, he was the most self-confident man I ever encountered."[85]

President Truman playing poker with his White House counsel, Clark Clifford, aboard the presidential yacht, July 4, 1949 (Margaret Truman Daniels Papers, Harry S. Truman Presidential Library, 81-154-04).

Over determined military resistance, Clifford now slipped a brief section creating a Central Intelligence Agency into the defense bill negotiated by Leahy. Although Truman and his national security adviser, Souers, would later fiercely deny this, the section included what Clifford called a "carefully phrased" catchall directive well understood by both the president and a handful of the most powerful congressional leaders that the CIA "shall perform such other functions and duties related to intelligence affecting the national security of the United States as the [president's] National Security Council may from time to time direct." According to Clifford, the new CIA would thus be charged with carrying out the same kinds of propaganda and covert political and even paramilitary activities that the OSS had conducted against the Nazis and Japanese, and that the Soviet Union and its Chinese and Korean allies were using against the West.[86] Regarding the CIA's secret powers, Massachusetts Democratic congressman, and later Speaker of the House, John McCormack said, "Those . . . in charge are doing what they ought to do for the country. I would not want to know all about it."[87] Most members of Congress agreed.

On the day that Rear Admiral Hillenkoetter was nominated to replace him, DCI Vandenberg urged Congress to enact the National Security Act to spare the United States the humiliation of having "to go, hat in hand, begging any foreign government for the eyes—the foreign intelligence—with which to see." He reminded Congress that early in World War II, "for months we had to rely blindly and trustingly on the superior intelligence of the British." Vandenberg continued that the United States must have a vigorous CIA "if we are to be forewarned against possible acts of aggression and if we are to be armed against disaster in an era of atomic warfare." He denounced the idea that there is anything "un-American about espionage and even about intelligence generally. We are a great world power and all great powers have strong intelligence systems."[88]

Truman's beloved mother, Martha, died back in Missouri as the president signed the National Security Act on July 26, 1947. In some ways the weak product of bitter departmental feuds and hard-won compromise, the Act protected the navy and Marine Corps, created a new air force and a weak secretary of defense with no staff, a Joint Chiefs of Staff (JCS) with no chairman, a CIA with a deliberately vague charter but a clear prohibition on domestic spying or *Gestapo* police powers, and a National Security Council (NCS) made up of the secretaries of State and Defense to advise the president on foreign policy and to direct the CIA. Most important, however, the president sat as chairman of the NSC, and the CIA was an independent agency reporting directly to him. Truman appointed the Act's fiercest opponent, Secretary of the Navy James Forrestal, as the first

President Truman, Secretary of the Navy James Forrestal, and Fleet Admiral Chester Nimitz, April 22, 1946, aboard the aircraft carrier *Franklin D. Roosevelt* (Edwin A. Locke Jr. Papers, Harry S. Truman Presidential Library, 63-308).

secretary of this National Military Establishment. In Clifford's words, Truman's "motives in choosing Forrestal were simple: if Forrestal remained Secretary of the Navy he would make life unbearable for the Secretary of Defense; if on the other hand he was the Secretary, he would have to make the system work."[89]

Bradley, who, after his tour as army chief of staff, would become the first Chairman of the Joint Chiefs in 1949, described Forrestal as "Irish. Not glad-handing or hard drinking, but reclusive, brooding, intense."[90] Forrestal soon admitted to the president that he had been wrong to try to weaken the Defense Establishment, and in 1949 a Reorganization Act strengthened the position of secretary of defense and created a chairmanship for the JCS.

Unfortunately, many weaknesses in the powers of the Director of Central Intelligence remained, and DCIs were never able to exercise the control over the military intelligence services that Clifford had intended.[91] Forrestal's former business friend Souers became executive secretary of the new National Security Council, making him, in effect, the president's most intimate foreign affairs and national security adviser. Souers, still anxious to return to private life in Saint Louis, took the job as a "personal favor" to Truman. At the end of the Truman presidency, still in the White House as "Special Consultant to the president," Souers was awarded the Distinguished Service Medal for his service, using his "vast knowledge of the problem of national security and his marked ability to achieve cooperation among all groups . . . to successfully integrate the functions of the [National Security] Council with those of other government agencies."[92]

According to the *New York Times*, Souers was surprised to receive the medal and asked the president, "Is that me you were talking about?"[93] In a warm editorial, the *Washington Post* called him "this selfless and dedicated man" who

President Truman awards the Distinguished Service Medal to National Security Council Executive Secretary Rear Admiral Sidney Souers, December 1, 1952 (Photograph by Abbie Rowe, National Park Service, Harry S. Truman Presidential Library, 73-3936).

"has known how to stay in the background, consulting and offering advice when called upon, but never intruding himself. A self-seeker or egoist could not have succeeded in such a job."[94] Souers himself told the *New York Times* that the National Security Advisor:

> Must be objective and willing to subordinate his personal views on policy to his task of coordinating the views of all responsible officials. He must remember at all times that in his position he shares neither the responsibility nor the authority which is vested in the [National Security] council as a body or its members as individuals. He should never take sides on any policy issue, since this would jeopardize his role as a neutral coordinator. He must be willing to forego publicity and personal aggrandizement.[95]

Remarkably, none of the men chosen to create and lead Harry Truman's evolving CIA wanted the job, and the first two, Admiral Souers and General Vandenberg, left as quickly as they could. As Hoyt Vandenberg returned to the army air force with his eyes firmly fixed on a new independent United States Air Force, he was replaced in May 1947 by brand-new Rear Admiral Roscoe Hillenkoetter, freshly returned from a year in Paris with a French Legion of Honor award.

Rear Admiral Roscoe Hillenkoetter, US naval attaché, Paris, awarded the French Legion of Honor, March 1947 (National Archives College Park, 306-NT-93B-33, courtesy of the *New York Times* Paris Bureau).

Although much junior to distinguished Secretary of State and General of the Army George Marshall, Fleet Admiral William Leahy, and formidable men such as future Secretary of Defense James Forrestal, Hillenkoetter was well respected by Leahy and Forrestal, both for his sea service and his intelligence experience as naval attaché and Pacific Fleet intelligence chief. His background and amiability did not, however, protect him from the same fierce opposition faced by his predecessors. Although the authors of the OSS War Report and former OSS officers were speaking of challenges faced by Donovan years earlier, once Hillenkoetter became DCI, the other agencies again "forgot their . . . animosities and joined in an attempt to strangle this unwanted newcomer at birth." "Many in Washington . . . knew what [the OSS and now the CIA] should be prevented from doing."[96]

From his days as a plebe at the naval academy, "Hilley" was admired for his intelligence and cheerfulness. In the sarcastic words of the senior-class yearbook:

President Truman witnessing Chief Justice D. Lawrence Groner (*second from left*) swearing in Rear Admiral Sidney Souers (*second from right*) as executive secretary of the National Security Council and Rear Admiral Roscoe Hillenkoetter (*far right*) as director of the Central Intelligence Agency, September 26, 1947. Also being sworn in is Arthur Hill (*center*), as chairman of the National Security Resources Board (Harry S. Truman Presidential Library, 59-1363).

"'Hilley's' overwhelming laziness is redeemed only by the fact that he is always willing to help any one not so fortunate" and "His shipmates and friends know that he is versatile and willing to do his share in everything."[97] Still trying to be accommodating decades later, he initially extended a peace offering to the hostile and defensive naval and army intelligence services by surrendering Hoyt Vandenberg's claim that the DCI could act as "executive agent," speaking for the secretaries of state, war, and the navy. He did this in June 1947 in the presence of the secretaries themselves, along with Admiral Leahy, "to create better feeling" with the army and navy intelligence chiefs just one month before Truman signed the National Security Act, creating the new National Security Council and CIA.[98] Hillenkoetter was ready to welcome advice, and even dissent from CIA judgements, but he reserved the right to sit as "observer, counsel, or advisor" to the NSC and make recommendations to the secretaries and president.[99] It soon became apparent, however, that his military intelligence rivals had every intention of trying to cripple and obstruct his authority, much as they had frustrated General Vandenberg by delaying his National Intelligence Estimates and fighting his effort to gain statutory authority for his agency and for himself as director. Since the soft sell wasn't working, Hilly finally deployed a big stick in a meeting he described as "one of the dramatic moments of his life."[100] Considering that Hillenkoetter had witnessed Nazi armies marching into a conquered Paris and had a battleship sink under him at Pearl Harbor, that is a remarkable statement. In early December 1947, in the office of new Secretary of Defense Forrestal—with the secretaries of the three military services, their intelligence chiefs, a State Department representative, and the Executive Secretary of the new National Security Council Sidney Souers all in attendance—Hillenkoetter explained his view of the CIA's role and authority under the NSC. Allowing no one else to speak, Forrestal turned directly to the chiefs of army and naval intelligence: "You are not going to interfere . . . . It is going to run as Hillenkoetter says. Do you both understood that now?" As Chief of Naval Intelligence Admiral Inglis later told Hillenkoetter: "He talked to us like a couple of plebes. I guess that makes us your servants now."[101] In a meeting with Inglis and his army colleague several days later, CIA General Counsel Lawrence Houston said that the DCI's "demeanor was as strong as [Houston] ever saw him use." The military services now had their orders, but Hillenkoetter and his new Agency still faced powerful domestic challengers, as well as daunting foreign threats to the United States and its fledgling national intelligence service.

The CIA, Roscoe Hillenkoetter, and the Cold War

Germany

ACCORDING TO EARLY MILITARY INTELLIGENCE and CIA official James Critchfield: "During those early years . . . the Army G-2, the director of naval intelligence, and . . . the director of central intelligence were all far too preoccupied with the [Washington] struggle over the restructuring of national intelligence to be involved with what was going on in intelligence . . . overseas."[1] In the words of the editorial director of Yale University Press:

> [What we see in these early postwar years] is a picture of two systems in action. The American intelligence system at the end of World War II had few professional or administrative resources. It was largely an ad hoc affair—poorly funded, poorly staffed, and without a secure future. By contrast in 1945 the Soviet intelligence service was a highly professional bureaucracy with a history going back to the 1917 Revolution.[2]

Germany had been the primary enemy during the world war that had just ended, and now the shattered capital city of Berlin was the laboratory that many hoped would be a model for Four Power cooperation in future relations between the Western democracies and the Soviet Union.[3] Although Germany had formally surrendered on May 8, 1945, the US Army Second Armored Division ("Hell on Wheels") was not allowed to enter Berlin until July 4. As part of Operation TORCH in November 1942, the division had landed in North Africa, where the new OSS had helped prepare the way for the first American counterattack against the Nazis. Now the soldiers were accompanied by Allen Dulles, OSS chief for Germany. Three months earlier Dulles had reported from Bern, Switzerland, that die-hard fanatic Nazis were gathering in an Alpine redoubt in southeastern Bavaria near Hitler's heavily guarded Berchtesgaden vacation compound. In fact, because the Germans most feared the advancing Soviets, determined to exact revenge for Nazi atrocities, the demoralized and broken German army and citizenry were no longer seriously resisting the Western allies. Colonel Critchfield, then a combat commander, considered "the totality of the German acceptance of defeat and unconditional surrender . . . quite remarkable."[4] The whole country was in chaos, with no civil order or transport, no utilities like electricity or heat, and no means of distributing food. The Western armies were equally unprepared to feed, house, or even control the population—or the six million displaced persons fleeing westward, or the hordes of former inmates of German concentration or prisoner-of-war camps. So many men were either dead or captured that Europe was literally a continent of women and orphans, with fifty-three thousand lost children in Berlin alone.[5] Many Russian prisoners of war or Red Army defectors did not want to return to Soviet control, adding to the pressure on US Army resources. Indeed, the best-organized relief effort was created by Jewish groups working to transport Jewish concentration camp survivors to Palestine.

Having liberated horrifying camps like Dachau near Munich and Mauthausen near Salzburg, most US troops were sympathetic to these Jewish efforts, despite British Army attempts to block the movement of survivors to their British Arab protectorate.[6]

US Army counterintelligence troops, soon augmented by former OSS members of the Strategic Services Unit (SSU), initially concentrated on denazification, finding and detaining former senior German military and civilian officials. President Truman had left Potsdam with the understanding that the United States was now the leader of a group of gravely weakened European allies, but he and Supreme Allied Commander General Dwight Eisenhower initially thought they could work directly with their Soviet counterparts. They didn't understand how firmly Stalin and the Communist Party controlled every aspect of state, including the Red Army. In an effort to be conciliatory, in fact, Eisenhower's deputy military governor for Germany, Lieutenant General Lucius Clay, made an agreement to return Red Army defectors—an action his intelligence subordinates would sometimes ignore as it became evident that the Soviets intended to loot any surviving German factories, abduct German scientists, and subvert noncommunist political parties. The United States was rapidly demobilizing, having discharged a million and a half troops every month and cut the defense budget by 80 percent.[7] By the end of 1945 the SSU was cut to two thousand, and Allen Dulles returned to his New York law practice, to be replaced by another future DCI, Richard Helms.[8]

Young Jewish Buchenwald survivors from Poland, Latvia, and Hungary on their way to Palestine, June 5, 1945 (National Archives College Park, "War and Conflict" album, photo 1262, US Army Signal Corps 1860-1985, RG111, ID 531300).

In Critchfield's view, "Stalin did not believe the United States was prepared to install itself as a long-term significant power in Europe."[9] Considering that the Soviets had lost some twenty-seven million in the war, compared to America's three hundred thousand, he also believed that the Soviet Union had earned the right to the lion's share of the spoils of victory.[10]

Stalin proved wrong about America's intent and quickly Army Intelligence expanded from chasing Nazis to watching the Soviets, especially their economic and political moves in their East German occupation zone. The Russians forced the East German democratic leftist Socialist Party to join the Red "Socialist Unity Party" and harassed the conservative Christian Democrats. Robert Murphy, who

Allen Dulles (*center*), Strategic Services Unit German chief, and colleagues, including his successor as director of central intelligence, Richard Helms (*far right*), Fall 1945 (Courtesy of the CIA).

had served with attaché Commander Roscoe Hillenkoetter in Paris in 1940, was now American ambassador in Berlin and read the political reports from the army's Berlin Operations Base (BOB) with great interest.[11]

Of even greater interest were Soviet efforts to develop an atomic bomb using uranium from East German and Czech mines, captured German scientists, and forced labor. Almost from the creation of the American nuclear weapons program on the day before the Japanese attack on Pearl Harbor, senior US military leaders worried that Germany, famous for its brilliant scientists and engineers, might be ahead in the race for an atomic weapon.[12] Vannevar Bush—Roosevelt's, and later Truman's, chief scientific adviser—admitted to having no idea of German activities. Army Chief of Staff Marshall and Manhattan Project chief Brigadier General

Leslie Groves both felt that the military intelligence agencies and the OSS would not understand the importance of the information being sought, and Groves was dismayed that "there was considerably more friction between the various intelligence agencies [OSS, army G-2, and ONI] than . . . previously suspected."[13] Groves thus took personal control of American intelligence efforts targeted at Germany, although he did enlist Donovan's OSS, especially Allen Dulles in Bern, to locate specific German specialists and report on Allied bomb damage to facilities and research institutes. Once Allied forces landed in Europe, teams of scientists and intelligence officers accompanied the army to collect nuclear material, documents, or personnel. By December 1944 it was clear that there was no risk of a German bomb, but the United States and Great Britain were determined that France not acquire German secrets and so shipped uranium, heavy water, and even Werner Heisenberg, the leader of German nuclear research, to England. As intelligence scholar Jeffrey Richelson has noted, the effort against Germany was a "practice run" for the "far lengthier, more extensive, and more sophisticated" anti-Soviet program.[14]

Stalin appointed his notorious and feared security and intelligence chief Lavrenty Beria to head the atomic program, telling him to "build the bomb quickly and not count the cost."[15] Thanks to spies within the Manhattan Project, the Russians had the road map; they just needed machinery, raw materials, and experts. Informed by defectors interrogated by the army and its British allies, Western services were able to keep track of East German factories and block Western suppliers from selling critical materials to the Soviets. The United States also undertook Operation PAPERCLIP to identify German technical experts and bring them to the United States. Among these experts was Wernher von Braun, who had worked on the German V-2 ballistic missile program and was in many ways one of the fathers of the American space program.[16]

The greatest and most controversial American advantage—in what Critchfield called "the largest, most concentrated and intense intelligence war in history"— was the Gehlen Organization, often simply called "the Org." Beginning in 1943, with the expectation that Germany would be defeated and the great future struggle would be between the Soviet Union and the victorious Western powers, German Army Major General Reinhard Gehlen assembled the intelligence files and experts from his Foreign Armies East (or *Fremde Heere Ost*) with the intention of volunteering this "only comprehensive information on Soviet military power held anywhere by anyone in the entire world" to the United States. Gehlen thought he had one of the few assets that Germany could offer the United States for the coming global struggle, and he was right.[17] Without informing either the OSS or army counterintelligence, Eisenhower's chief of intelligence, Brigadier

General Edwin L. Sibert, created Operation RUSTY to use Gehlen's experience and expertise to gather as much intelligence as possible on the Soviet army, its organization, and its operations.[18] As one Army Intelligence officer remembered, "[We were] CIA, FBI, and military security all in one because those agencies weren't functioning in Germany at the time . . . we were achieving a minor miracle every day in getting as much information as we did."[19] To fund the Org's activities and pay its people, the army allowed it to sell scarce American goods, such as cigarettes, coffee, and chocolate on the black market.[20] The collection effort against the Soviet military was called GRAIL, and as David Murphy, later chief of the CIA's Berlin Base and then its Soviet Division, said, "Sibert plunged into this enormous mission with remarkable energy and determination." Some two hundred fifty spies worked on the effort, but because of poor Western security and very effective Soviet counterintelligence, most were caught and sent to Soviet Gulag labor camps before being freed in 1955, when the Soviets finally returned all German prisoners of war.[21] Indeed, the Americans were facing a ruthless and experienced adversary, and army efforts to recruit Germans or Soviet officers were frustrated by such techniques as "Pavlovsky's Trap," in which Red intelligence officers would pretend to be Americans to catch any Russians tempted to betray the paranoid Soviets.[22] Berlin was still a battleground, with 337 people kidnapped in June 1946, some 245 in the Soviet zone alone; many simply disappeared without a trace.[23]

The difficulties faced by the inexperienced and outnumbered American intelligence officers in Berlin were remarkable. Once Hoyt Vandenberg became DCI, field officers moved from the temporary army Strategic Services Unit into the new Central Intelligence Group, and then, under Hillenkoetter in 1947, into the CIA. In April 1948 the CIA Chief of Station Germany sent a lengthy message to Washington detailing the activities of Berlin Operations Base from January 1946 until just before the Berlin Blockade. In the face of fairly strong hostility from General Clay—and with an average of only forty officers, clerks, and support personnel—Berlin Base initially produced some five thousand intelligence reports a year, with more than five hundred alone produced in August 1947. Increased emphasis on quality, and a new focus on strategic reporting, dropped the numbers to a still-impressive two hundred reports a month thereafter. The rate of reporting also dropped because of devastating agent losses caused by haste, bad security practices, and tough Russian counterintelligence efficiency. It was extremely difficult to keep operations going in a ruined city. Among the most urgent requirements were housing for staff and agents and reliable transportation for field collection officers. The Base Chief described his motor pool as "unquestionably the aspect . . . in which I've been forced to take the closest personal interest." It was almost impossible for the base's German mechanics to keep their old, broken-down American and German "struggle buggys" running, until finally, in the spring of 1947, the British gave the base thirty new "bumble bee" Volkswagen Beetles from the VW factory in the British zone of West Germany.[24]

Still, the army was able to publish a weekly *Soviet Military Roundup* on the Red Army in Germany and the Central Intelligence Group and CIA were also producing increasingly sophisticated reports. As the US Army continued to withdraw, by February 1947, just before Hillenkoetter replaced Vandenberg as DCI, the Soviet army had a half million men in East Germany, compared to some one hundred fifty thousand American soldiers in West Germany. Neither the army nor the new CIA was completely comfortable with the Gehlen Org. In June 1947 Hillenkoetter recommended that the private intelligence agency be disbanded because of fears that Gehlen's officers carried too much Nazi baggage and might become the core of a new German General Staff like the highly skilled professional officers who had served the World War I *Kaiser* and World War II *Führer* so efficiently and ruthlessly. Gehlen survived, and in December 1947 the Org, now code-named *Nicholaus* for the German Christmas saint, moved to a former Nazi compound in the village of Pullach, just south of Munich, under US Army cover. Gehlen, known professionally by the alias "Dr. Schneider," continued to fund his activities with army black-market coffee and cigarettes.[25]

Berlin Blockade and Airlift

In early 1948 the Soviets shocked the few remaining American optimists by brutally seizing control of Czechoslovakia, the second time in a decade that a small, picturesque Central European country had fallen under the control of foreign aggressors. The Jewish state of Israel declared its independence from the British protectorate of Palestine and was immediately recognized by the United States. And Stalin turned up the pressure on the Allied foothold in Berlin as subject East Germans grew more restive. Just before Christmas 1947, Hillenkoetter's new CIA had warned policymakers that the Soviets might try to force the Western allies from Berlin, but the Russian intelligence service was too afraid to contradict Stalin's view that the Allies would withdraw under pressure.[26] In early March, military governor General Clay, whom US Army Chief of Staff Bradley called one of the "brightest, most quietly forceful generals," alarmed Washington by stating that "war may come with dramatic suddenness."[27] He had sent this assessment without consulting his new CIA Berlin Base, which responded that it saw "no reliable evidence that the USSR intends to resort to military action within the next sixty days."[28] Nonetheless, the Red Army increased its harassment of highways and rail traffic, and on April 6, 1948, a Soviet fighter collided with a British passenger aircraft, killing everybody aboard. A month later the KGB warned Stalin that General Clay was determined to hold West Berlin and would use fighters to escort American transport aircraft if necessary.[29] The crisis could not have come at a worse time. Determined to help Republican New York governor Thomas Dewey defeat Truman in the 1948 presidential election, the Republican Congress cut taxes, and the army was reduced to a half-million troops "serving as policemen or clerks," in the words of Army Chief of Staff General Bradley.[30]

By now General Clay, who was responsible for all of West Germany, had determined that economic recovery was impossible without currency reform. On June 20, 1948, as the Marshall Plan for American redevelopment aid was being discussed, Clay established the West or D-Mark (*deutsche Mark*), which became one of the world's strongest currencies until replaced fifty years later by the common Western European euro. Four days later the Soviets cut off electricity to West Berlin and closed all surface transit corridors between Berlin and West Germany. These actions angered East Germans, all of whom remembered how the Red Army had looted and raped its way into Berlin, and many of whom now volunteered to help the CIA. It also hurt East German industry, dependent upon West Berlin workers and western material. Without militarily challenging the surface blockade, General Clay ordered a massive airlift, which continued through the bitter German winter, bringing food, other supplies, and even coal to the surrounded city. As senior State Department officer George Kennan said, "The situation was dark and full of danger."[31] To everyone's surprise, the depleted American and British air forces responded magnificently.

On Easter Sunday in 1949, some 1,349 American and British transport flights reached West Berlin in a single day. CIA Berlin Base morale during the blockade was "never higher," with many wives of CIA officers working at the base, and they all felt that policymakers in Germany and Washington depended upon their reporting and analysis—which concluded that the Soviets would refrain from military action. On the Soviet side, KGB reporting was dangerously misleading about German and Allied resolve, encouraging Stalin to prolong the blockade. As a Soviet officer at KGB headquarters in Karlshorst in East Berlin concluded: "The blockade brought no benefit to the Soviet side, only damage. . . . It . . . arouse[d] the German population against us."[32] In General Bradley's words: "We were very lucky in the Berlin Blockade . . . the airlift turned out to be our single greatest triumph of the Cold War."[33]

In fact, from Stalin's perspective, the damage was much worse than simply further alienating Germans against the Soviets. A month before the end of the blockade, the Western Allies formed the North Atlantic Treaty Organization (NATO), which to this day unites Western military forces in defense of Europe and each

Barefoot German children watching an American air force C-54 landing in Berlin during the airlift (National Archives College Park, RG342-G, Box 25, folder F, misc, photo 83893).

other. In May 1949, the same month Stalin finally ended the blockade, a new constitution created the Federal Republic of Germany, with Bonn as its capital and West Berlin as its twelfth state. The United States and Great Britain agreed to combine their western occupation zones into a unified "Bizonia" and encouraged the re-arming of a West German federal military or *Bundeswehr.* Stalin of course saw this remilitarization as an offensive move by the West, aimed at the Soviet Union, rather than a defensive reaction to his own ill-advised policies.[14]

With the Berlin Airlift still underway, the chief of the CIA's new Munich base, James Critchfield, was directed by DCI Hillenkoetter in October 1948 to investigate the Gehlen Org and recommend whether the private intelligence service should be liquidated or taken over from the US Army by the CIA. The Org was strongly contributing to the success of the Allied Airlift by providing DUSTBIN communications intelligence on Soviet air force activities to airlift commander General Curtis LeMay.[15] Unaware that Hillenkoetter opposed the Org, Critchfield saw the desirability of future German-American intelligence cooperation and recommended Gehlen's activities continue. Accordingly, in July 1949 Critchfield was directed to assume CIA oversight, and seven years later, in February 1956, the Org became the German Federal Intelligence Service or *Bundesnachrichtend-ienst* (BND) of the Federal Republic.[36] The US high commissioner for Germany, John McCloy, who succeeded Lucius Clay as American viceroy, was not told of the army's association with the Org.[37] From the beginning, CIA and BND analysts worked closely and cooperatively on Soviet military issues, and this broad cooperation continued through the end of the Cold War and the re-unification of Germany in 1990.

Austria and the Rat Line

Although many Austrians welcomed the March 1938 *Anschluß* or incorporation into Hitler's German empire, the World War II Allies officially considered Austria to be Hitler's first victim. That did not mean, however, that at the end of the war, Austria was not held complicit in Nazi actions. Like Germany, in 1945, the small Alpine country was divided into four zones, with the capital, Vienna, like Berlin, governed by the victorious Four Powers. As in Germany, the Soviets exacted steep reparations in their occupation zone, confiscated factories, and worked hard to incite and recruit local communist activists. Like Berlin, Vienna also proved to be an excellent vantage point for American and British intelligence agencies to gather information on Soviet economic and political activities, not only in Austria but in all of Eastern Europe, including the ongoing Soviet subjugation of Poland, Czechoslovakia, Hungary, and Romania. US Army intelligence in Austria developed an elaborate system to identify and interrogate Soviet military defectors, Eastern European refugees, including Eastern European democratic politicians, forced laborers, and displaced persons. Like the Japanese prisoners of war interrogated in the Pacific by officers of Hillenkoetter's Pacific Fleet Intelligence Center, many Europeans had valuable insights and information about activities and conditions behind Stalin's new Iron Curtain and were willing to share this intelligence with American officials. Immediately after the war, Critchfield had been the chief of military intelligence in Vienna, but his operations chief, Major James Milano, worked out of American military headquarters in Salzburg in western Austria, near American-occupied Bavaria. As in Germany, American interrogators hid promising sources in temporary housing while they were questioned, but once these people had given all possible intelligence on the Soviets, the question arose as to what to do with them. General Clay, with Eisenhower's approval, had agreed to return all Soviets to the Red Army, but most volunteers obviously did not wish to be repatriated. To its credit, Army Intelligence felt a responsibility to these courageous men, who faced a life of slave labor or death were it discovered they had helped the Americans. In 1949, when both the Defense Department and the CIA were strengthened and given new authorities, the DCI was granted a maximum of one hundred visas a year to bring the most valuable secret agents into the United States. Most sources were by no means so valuable, and the US government did not want to assume permanent responsibility for them.[38] A number of other countries, including some in Latin America, were, however, willing to accept certain selected refugees. Without informing the State Department, or even their senior commanders, Milano's officers devised a system to forge new identities for them and smuggle these people into British-occupied Trieste in northeastern Italy, where a Croatian priest was willing to sell Latin American visas to "respectable Christians." It would later develop that among those who took advantage of this "rat line" to escape Europe were notorious German war criminals, but many others were simply informants seeking peaceful new lives.[39] Others passing through Vienna and Trieste were Jewish survivors of German death camps trying to reach Palestine. As Milano said, "The US military deliberately turned a blind eye"[40] to the flow of Jews and weapons to Zionist groups in Palestine, and in 1948 President Harry Truman was the first world leader to recognize the new Jewish state of Israel.

The CIA and Wars by Other Means

The Soviet takeover of Eastern Europe and the Berlin Blockade focused Washington's attention on events playing out on the "savage continent," but many battles were also being fought within the US government. In the spring of 1948, testifying in a secret hearing before the Senate and House Appropriations Committees, DCI Hillenkoetter told the members: "We thought . . . we would have time to develop this mature [CIA] over a period of years. . . . Unfortunately, the international situation has not allowed us the breathing space . . . we find ourselves in operations up to our neck."[41] He asked for authority to spend secret funds outside normal congressional oversight, and the Senate unanimously agreed, with only four House members voting against such spending. As Hillenkoetter's sole congressional liaison officer, Walter Pforzheimer, later remembered: "There were very loose reins on us . . . because the Congress believed in us and what we were doing. It wasn't that we were trying to hide anything. Our main problem was, we couldn't get them to sit still and listen."[42] A few months earlier, speaking of the bitter civil war in Greece, Massachusetts Republican senator Henry Cabot Lodge had said:

> I sometimes think we get a little bit too sensitive about interfering in the
> internal affairs of other countries. . . . The Russians . . . have gone about as

far as they can go in what they say . . . and whether we interfere or [not], they are going to accuse us of the most dreadful things. . . . We are in it up to our neck, and almost everybody . . . will be damned glad to see us interfere.

Democratic Senator Walter George of Georgia agreed: "Of course . . . I agree with you. We are going to have to run the whole show."[43]

While Congress might have been willing to pay the CIA's relatively modest budgets of $40 to $50 million in 1948 and 1949, even the Berlin Blockade did not keep them from making draconian cuts to the defense budget.[44] As General Bradley described the situation, with no money or troops, military planners were forced to rely on using the US nuclear and long-range bomber monopoly for a strategy of "massive retaliation" against the Soviets. This pleased the new United States Air Force, which was eager to have Congress buy it expensive new bombers, but it led the airmen to question the value of the navy's aircraft carriers and of the marines, since the Russians as a continental power had no significant navy and no islands to invade. In General Bradley's words, "An unseemly semi-public Air Force-Navy brawl ensued."[45] Following Truman's shocking victory over the confident Dewey in November 1948, Dean Acheson replaced General Marshall as secretary of state and James Forrestal was replaced as secretary of defense by Truman's incompetent political friend and fund-raiser Louis Johnson, who promptly canceled the plans to construct the navy's new supercarrier.

Bradley, as army chief of staff, was joined on the JCS by Hoyt Vandenberg of the air force and Admiral Louis Denfield as chief of naval operations. Bradley called Johnson "probably the worst appointment Truman made during his presidency" and considered both him and Forrestal mentally ill.[46] Three months after the Berlin Blockade finally ended in May 1949, General Bradley was made chairman of the JCS, and what had been the simmering rivalry between the air force and navy over scarce funds exploded into what Bradley called an "utterly disgraceful . . . completely dishonest" admirals' revolt and smear campaign against the air force's new A-bomb–carrying long-range strategic B-36 bomber. Bradley was outraged by the "crybaby" attitude of naval aviators and marines who wanted to protect their aircraft carriers and, in public testimony on Capitol Hill, called the admirals "fancy Dans" unwilling to be team players.[47] With the military so weak that its commanders thought they could only defeat the huge Red Chinese and Soviet armies with nuclear weapons, the only other choice seemed to be diplomacy. But American leaders doubted Stalin would honor any treaties or agreements he might make. Still, in his Truman Doctrine, the president had promised that the United States "would support free peoples."[48]

President Truman greets Secretary of Defense Louis Johnson at Washington National Airport, December 20, 1949, with Secretary of State Dean Acheson (*far left*) and Secretary of the Interior Oscar Chapman (*between Truman and Johnson*) (Harry S. Truman Presidential Library, 73-3268).

At that moment, therefore, senior Washington officials seemed to agree that it would be better to fight communist aggression and subversion with the kind of shadow warriors that the wartime OSS and British Special Operations Executive had deployed just a few years earlier, rather than the massive numbers of increasingly costly new weapons that the military wanted. But since even "Wild Bill" Donovan had agreed that special covert operations were inappropriate for a peacetime national intelligence organization, and since most of the trained and experienced covert operators had been dismissed when Truman abolished the OSS, who in the US government would now direct, manage, and deploy these "agents of influence"?

Interestingly enough, the government agency most eager to do so was the Department of State, and the man arguing most strongly for covert action was Milwaukee-born George Kennan. His "Long Telegram" from Moscow in February 1946 described a Soviet "elaborate and far-flung operation for exertion of . . .

influence in other countries . . . managed by people whose experience and skill in underground methods are . . . without parallel in history."[49] General Marshall was deeply impressed and, once he became secretary of state in 1947, appointed Kennan his chief of policy planning—in effect, head of his internal think tank. Kennan saw the need for an equally aggressive, skillfully managed American effort but had an "unconcealed low opinion" of DCI Hillenkoetter and what he saw as "ineffectual, limited CIA operations."[50] In the words of one scholar, "Many State Department leaders wanted to control the CIA but avoid blame if things went wrong." The very first National Security Council Directive, in November 1947, was Truman's first move to fulfill the Truman Doctrine promise to support free people, in this case non-Communist Italian political parties. Using $10 million in secret confiscated Nazi money, the CIA supported democratic Italian parties and unions, paid for newspapers and other "psychological warfare" propaganda, paid bribes, and helped defeat the Communists in national elections. According to distinguished intelligence scholar Christopher Andrew, Truman sent Hillenkoetter his personal congratulations after the Christian Democrats won the vote.[51]

The NSC continued to encourage this shadow warfare. In mid-December 1947, it agreed that because of "the vicious psychological efforts of the USSR . . . to discredit and defeat the aims and activities of the US . . . in the interests of world peace and US national security, [public US activities like diplomacy and the Marshall Plan] must be supplemented by [CIA] covert operations."[52] By the

President Truman (*second from right*) and the National Security Council, August 19, 1948: Secretary of State and General of the Army George C. Marshall (*third from right*), NSC Executive Secretary Rear Admiral Souers (*third from left*), DCI Rear Admiral Hillenkoetter (*fifth from the left*), and Secretary of Defense James Forrestal (*fourth from right*) (Photograph by Abbie Rowe, National Park Service, Harry S. Truman Presidential Library, 73-2704).

middle of 1948, Kennan's Policy Planning Staff, "in an atmosphere of near panic" over the Berlin Blockade, recommended a new "covert political warfare operations directorate within the government [to conduct 'covert operations.']"[53] In mid-June 1948, the National Security Council issued the famous NSCD 10/2, which essentially defined covert action (CA):

> Specifically, such operations shall include any covert activities related to propaganda: preventive direct action including sabotage . . . demolition . . . subversion against hostile states, including assistance to underground resistance movements, guerrillas and refugee liberation groups, and support of indigenous anti-communist elements in threatened countries of the free world.

And most important, if those secret CA operations should be discovered, "The US government can plausibly [deny] any responsibility for them."[54] Even General Donovan's OSS, in the darkest days of World War II, did not have such an expansive worldwide charter. To carry out this NSC Directive, since neither Secretary Marshall nor Secretary Forrestal wanted CA in their departments, a compromise was reached with a reluctant DCI Hillenkoetter, under which the CIA would provide "quarters and rations" or office space, funding, and staff, while Kennan's Policy Planning Staff would provide policy guidance.[55] Allen Dulles, who was advising Thomas Dewey in his attacks on the Truman administration and expecting to become Dewey's DCI, declined the job to lead this new office, so Kennan turned to another OSS veteran, the Mississippi-born son of a wealthy logging family, Frank Wisner.

A graduate of the University of Virginia, Wisner was intense, restless, and full of high moral purpose. As an OSS officer stationed briefly in Bucharest, Romania, during the war, he organized a daring operation to fly B-17 bombers into Bucharest to rescue seventeen hundred American aircrew prisoners of war on August 29, 1944, as the German Army retreated before the oncoming Red Army. His hatred of the Soviets arose from watching the Red Army deport minority ethnic German *Volksdeutsche*, many of whom had lived in Transylvania for generations, to Russian labor camps, something he called the "most profound influence of his life."[56] According to OSS sergeant Arthur Schlesinger Jr., later a famous historian and presidential adviser, "He was already mobilizing for the Cold War. . . . [Frank] was a little excessive, even for me."[57] By 1946 he was again at a New York law firm, where he and his friend Allen Dulles "were pining to get back. . . . They were like fighter pilots. . . . They were both great romantics and saw themselves as the saviors of the world."[58] Initially, Wisner was brought back to the

State Department by Acheson to work with the seven hundred thousand Eastern European refugees then in Germany, many of whom had fought with the Nazis against the Red Army as it overran their countries. These hardened soldiers were seen as a potential secret army that could be sent back behind the Iron Curtain, just as OSS teams had penetrated European countries occupied by the Nazis. The Italian election experience had shown that émigré political groups, labor unions, and noncommunist leftist parties could be mobilized on behalf of the West. As OSS veteran and future CIA director William Colby remembered, Wisner and his colleagues worked in "the atmosphere of an order of Knights Templar, to save Western freedom from Communist darkness."[59] As Wisner himself said, "It is possible to avert a third world war by drastic actions of an affirmative character short of war."[60]

Wisner told Richard Bissell, a Yale economist then working on the Marshall Plan but later an innovative CIA senior officer, that his new, innocently named CIA Office of Policy Coordination (OPC) was being funded, with President Truman's approval, with foreign contributions to Marshall Fund monies.[61] Once the Berlin Blockade began, the Defense Department urged Wisner to recruit "stay behind" sabotage teams to remain in areas overrun by the Soviets and be prepared to act should the Red army attack Western Europe. OPC, with US Army cooperation, buried radios, weapons, explosives, and gold coins to be used in emergency by these teams; as late as the 1990s, such caches were occasionally uncovered in Austria and Germany. Wisner hired flamboyant State Department veteran Carmel Offie, Hillenkoetter's old 1940 Paris Embassy colleague, to recruit suitable fighters from among the refugees. Some were Nazis, and in the words of an early CIA officer: "We knew what we were doing. It was a visceral business of using any bastard as long as he was anti-communist."[62] Beyond the stay-behinds, OPC trained five thousand "post-nuclear guerrilla forces" and teams to be parachuted into occupied countries like Ukraine and the Baltic republics, where anti-Soviet armed bands were still hiding in thick forests.[63] In April 1949 Wisner and the British Intelligence Service decided to conduct a "clinical test" on the possibility of "rolling back" Communist control of Albania. The British Secret Intelligence Service (SIS) officer in Washington working with Wisner was Harold "Kim" Philby, who had, along with a number of his fellow Cambridge University students, been recruited by the KGB in the 1930s. The Albanians, forewarned, were waiting to ambush the OPC teams. The same fate awaited teams in other countries, and ruthless Soviet internal security proved impossible to penetrate. The Russians also kidnapped or assassinated resistance leaders living in the West.[64] DCI Hillenkoetter was not alone among CIA officers in his unhappiness with Wisner and the OPC, which had been walled off as a separate organization from the classic espionage and collection function of CIA's Office of Special Operations(OSO). As an OSO Berlin Base officer recalled: "The OPCers had that missionary zeal in their eyes. We distrusted missionary zeal."[65]

The CIA also distrusted the émigrés and refugees so enthusiastically recruited by Carmel Offie. In a memo to NSC Executive Director Sidney Souers, on April 19, 1948—entitled "Utilization of the Mass of Soviet Refugees"—Hillenkoetter warned Souers that the CIA had learned quite a lot about the refugees themselves while interrogating and debriefing them for intelligence on the Red Army and conditions in Eastern Europe. What the CIA had learned were the same painful lessons learned repeatedly by the OSS in trying to navigate the rival factions and local animosities to rally resistance to the Japanese in China and the Germans in Europe during World War II:

> These groups are highly unstable and undependable, split by personal rivalries and ideological differences, and primarily concerned with developing a secure position for themselves. . . . They . . . are rarely able to tap useful sources of information within the USSR, and generally concentrate on producing highly biased propaganda materials in place of objective intelligence. . . . They are almost exclusively interested in obtaining maximum support (usually from the U.S.) for their own . . . activities and insist upon the provision of substantial financial, communications, propaganda . . . and personal assistance in return for vague and unrealistic promises of future service.[66]

By bragging about US support, the refugees immediately attracted Russian attention and penetration by Soviet counterintelligence. Hillenkoetter acknowledged that some émigrés might be useful in wartime but recommended great caution in their use.[67] Wisner and his Knights Templar were not, however, cautious men.

Hillenkoetter's warnings proved equally prescient in the Far East, where General Stillwell and the OSS had been bitterly disappointed by Chiang Kai-shek's Chinese Nationalists. Immediately after World War II, President Truman had asked General Marshall to try to resolve the conflict between Mao's Red Army and the Nationalists, the latter of whom had, by 1949, been pushed off the mainland to the island of Taiwan. From its base in Taiwan, OPC bought Flying Tiger hero Claire Chennault's Civil Air Transport and conspired with Chennault and Chiang to drop teams and supplies into China to destabilize the Communist regime. Ironically, the first CIA officer killed in action was not one of Wisner's shadow warriors but a classic undercover intelligence collector: Douglas Mackiernan.

Experienced as a meteorologist in China, and based there as a State Department consul, one of Mackiernan's missions was to watch the Soviet nuclear program. Once the Communists seized control of the Chinese mainland, he tried to escape south through Tibet but was killed by Tibetan soldiers who had not yet learned that they were supposed to protect him.[68] When the Korean War broke out a few months later, three hundred OPC officers trained and funded eighty-five hundred Nationalist guerrillas. They also dropped propaganda leaflets and broadcast anti-Mao radio messages. They even conducted some eighteen raids, trying to link up with the five hundred thousand anti-Mao fighters that Chiang claimed were on the mainland. These raids were as unsuccessful as the anti-Mao fighters were imaginary.[69]

Despite repeated disappointment, Congress continued to support Covert Action. As a British critic of the program observed, "There was little public inclination to question the wisdom or the ethics of the means by which government officials conducted the Cold War."[70] Former congressional staffer and senior CIA official Britt Snider agreed: "[Congress] had set up the CIA to work secretly against the spread of communism, and they were not about to let a [chaotic] Congress interfere with that mission."[71] As CIA legislative counsel Walter Pforzheimer said, most members did not want to know details. They deferred to a small group of powerful senior chairmen, and there was remarkable bipartisan consensus and support for the agency. In 1949 OPC had 302 staff and 7 overseas posts, but by 1952, in the midst of the Korean War, it had 2,812 headquarters staff plus 3,142 overseas contractors in 47 posts. From an overall budget of $50 million in fiscal year 1949, Truman's last CIA budget request for fiscal year 1953 was $587 million. In 1952 the OPC budget alone was $82 million.[72] While the CIA budget was hidden in the larger budgets of the Defense and State Departments, Congress referred to Covert Action as "cold war activities" in its budget documents.[73]

Give 'Em Hell, Hilly

Walter Trohan, the outspoken conservative reporter for the anti-Truman *Chicago Tribune*—which had printed his 1945 stories accusing Donovan of trying to turn the OSS into a postwar "super *Gestapo* agency,"[74]—later said of Truman: "[He] wasn't a great guy for deceit . . . it was part of his code to defend everybody in his organization."[75] Truman was famous for his loyalty and direct plain speaking, but also for reacting with anger to criticism of his family, friends, and government colleagues. One of his campaign aides recalled that during the president's marathon whistle-stop train tour in the bitter and hard-fought 1948 national election against Republican Thomas Dewey, people in the crowds assembled to hear him speak from the rear platform of the train would shout "Give 'em hell, Harry." Truman would reply, "I'm not going to give 'em hell but just tell . . . the truth." Writing in 1960, he elaborated: "I have never deliberately given anybody hell. I just tell the truth on the opposition—and they think its hell."[76]

As a good naval officer, Roscoe Hillenkoetter shared many of those same impulses: loyalty to his "troops," straightforward truth-telling, and taking responsibility for his actions as well as his "crew." For him, as much as for Truman, "the buck stopped here." At Pearl Harbor, his after-action report gave full credit to the heroic individual initiative of his junior officers in saving *West Virginia* from capsizing as it settled to the harbor bottom. *Oklahoma,* moored next to *West Virginia* in Battleship Row, was not so fortunate and rolled over as she sank with much greater loss of life. He did not try to exaggerate his own role to gain any commendation beyond the Purple Heart awarded to him. Five years later, in January 1946, now in command of the celebrated *Missouri,* Captain Hillenkoetter returned to his hometown of Saint Louis leading a delegation of sailors, including another Missouri-born African American mess steward like the famous Dorie Miller (who had won a Navy Cross for his heroic defense of *West Virginia* at Pearl Harbor).

Captain Roscoe Hillenkoetter and battleship *Missouri* crewmen, Saint Louis, January 1946 (*St. Louis Globe-Democrat,* January 6, 1946, collection of the St. Louis Mercantile Library).

The Saint Louis Jewish Council of B'nai B'rith hosted a party for the sailors at one of the most elegant hotels in town, but hotel management tried to exclude the black sailor. Hillenkoetter announced: "He's a member of the crew. . . . If he doesn't come, we don't come."[77] And all the sailors went to the party with their captain.

Hillenkoetter, who was apparently happiest on the bridge of a warship or serving as a military attaché, brought the same sense of duty, commitment, good humor, and righteous anger to the position of DCI that he had brought to the assignment as chief of Admiral Nimitz's Intelligence Center, Pacific Ocean Area (ICPOA) five years earlier. And in both cases he faced similar intractable challenges. At Pearl Harbor he was up to his neck in war, and at the CIA he was up to his neck in espionage operations in the Cold War. In each case he fought against a fearsome foreign enemy without any time to catch his breath; gather a well-trained, experienced, and competent staff; or develop a clear strategy for his ramshackle organization or the war it was facing. And in neither case were all the enemies on the other side of the ocean. At Pearl Harbor Hillenkoetter replaced brilliant Commander Joseph Rochefort, brought down by jealous fellow navy officers, and in Washington he replaced a wealthy senior businessman and a glamorous and well-connected air force general—both of whom couldn't wait to leave the job he was taking over from them. Souers was a smooth facilitator with a sharp tongue who wished to leave government, and Vandenberg an impatient young man with his eye on a completely different fledgling organization he hoped to shape. Upon his appointment as director, Hillenkoetter received a handwritten note of congratulations from one of his ICPOA workers, reminding him of their time together in the months after Pearl Harbor at "that mistrusted stepchild of the Pacific." The director responded, "It would have been more exact if you had sent condolences. However, we shall try to make the thing work." Three days later, Souers sent the new director a warm letter expressing confidence that he would "do a swell job in a very difficult situation."[78]

Hillenkoetter thus clearly recognized that he was again assuming command in 1947 of a struggling organization, with most of its best and most-skilled men and women long since departed and most of its offices woefully understaffed. Much of his time in those early months was devoted to dealing personally with job seekers.[79] The CIA, nonetheless, immediately had to engage in a life-and-death shadow war against a ruthless and much more experienced Soviet intelligence adversary. And beyond that, the CIA was now charged with penetrating the Iron Curtain and advising the president and his administration on the military, economic, and covert capabilities of the Soviet Union and its allies and captive states. Not only was it impossible to assess accurately just what forces and weapons

Stalin might possess, it was even harder to penetrate what Chip Bohlen called the dictator's "talent for disguise" and fully understand the "harsh and brutal nature behind his mask."[80] Both Soviet capabilities and intentions were carefully and effectively hidden. Even George Kennan—the acclaimed diplomatic Kremlin watcher whose "Long Telegram" and subsequent "Mr. X" article earned General Marshall's respect and galvanized Washington policymakers, with their call for "containing" the Soviets—soon worried that his careful assessments were being perverted into policies that would dangerously antagonize Stalin.[81] The CIA was supposed to be the authoritative source of national judgments on foreign capabilities and intentions, but hostility and obstructionism from other government agencies was making that mission impossible. In late 1947 the Defense Department's legendary science adviser, Vannevar Bush, who had been instrumental in both the Manhattan Project and the development of early computers, warned Secretary Forrestal that the CIA was "completely stymied" in collecting scientific intelligence for the American Atomic Energy Commission (AEC) on Soviet nuclear developments because of lack of cooperation from the military services.[82]

Hillenkoetter's enemies, including OPC chief Frank Wisner, who officially worked for him, considered him an "amiable lightweight," but he was initially well respected by Admiral Leahy, Secretary Forrestal, members of Congress, and even Washington journalists.[83] While generally trying hard to keep the CIA out of the press, he was soon on a first-name "Hilly and Joe" basis with the formidable and influential columnist Joseph Alsop. By cultivating elite journalists, he was able "by special plea of the Director" to keep such powerful magazines and newspapers as *Life, Time, Newsweek, US News,* and the *New York Herald* from printing specific stories on subjects the CIA wished to keep hidden.[84] Again, while trying hard to limit interaction with Congress, Hillenkoetter and his senior managers periodically briefed committees on the Soviet Union. They were not willing to send written reports to Congress because only the Joint Atomic Energy Committee could store secret information, but since the CIA was one of the few sources on Russia, members welcomed the briefings.[85] Once the National Security Act made Hillenkoetter the statutory DCI, he was reconfirmed unanimously. In general, as Pforzheimer and a number of members of Congress said, they didn't want to know too much about CIA activities, but they were concerned about public "failures." In such cases, "Congress would hold the Director personally responsible and look no further."[86] Thanks to secrecy, most operational failures, such as the loss of agents trying to penetrate the Soviet Union or China, were unknown either to Congress or most Americans, but some events were so public that everybody read about them, critics denounced them, and Congress demanded answers.

President Truman with General of the Army George C. Marshall (*right*) and Dean Acheson (*left*), December 26, 1950 (Harry S. Truman Presidential Library, 60-42).

The first such event took place in April 1948 while Secretary of State Marshall was visiting Bogota, Colombia.[87] The unexpected assassination of a local politician led to riots that threatened Marshall's motorcade. Republican presidential candidate Dewey, being advised by Allen Dulles, criticized the administration, with Truman admitting he was "as surprised as anyone." DCI Hillenkoetter was summoned to testify about this "intelligence failure," although he warned Republican senator Robert Taft of Ohio that the hearings would backfire against the critics.[88] Arming himself, as was his custom, with CIA reports about the situation, Hillenkoetter read from reports that had been passed to the American ambassador but not forwarded to Washington so as not to "unduly alarm" the secretary. The chairman apologized to Hillenkoetter then took him out into the corridor to apologize again in front of reporters, saying, "CIA performed its duty." The State Department was furious that the CIA had revealed its warnings to Congress, but Hillenkoetter responded that the State Department "deserved whatever heat might now be on them." Further, he threatened to complain to

President Truman and Congress if cooperation between the State Department and the CIA on a host of issues didn't improve.[89]

The next failure, and one of the most critical events of the entire Cold War, was the detonation of the first Soviet atomic bomb in late summer 1949. In Jeffrey Richelson's words, "While US intelligence agencies would provide no advance warning . . . it was not for lack of trying."[90] As we now know from VENONA US Army decryption of KGB messages about its American spies, the Soviets had thoroughly penetrated both the American and British nuclear weapons programs, and they had stolen the secret of the bomb's design.[91] In 1949 American policymakers knew that the Russians were feverishly trying to build an atomic bomb. American intelligence and the Gehlen Org were trying to block Soviet efforts to use German scientists and East German uranium in the endeavor, and the CIA and British SIS were trying to understand what lay hidden behind the Iron Curtain. Refugees and returning prisoners of war could identify general locations of suspected nuclear facilities, but as DCI Hillenkoetter told President Truman in July 1948, "It continues to be impossible to determine the exact status of or determine the date . . . for the completion of their first atomic bomb."[92] Vannevar Bush had warned Secretary of Defense Forrestal that the CIA was "stymied," and as late as April 1949, DCI Hillenkoetter asked NSC Executive Secretary Souers for increased military communications intercepts to monitor Russian facilities and activities. The Joint Chiefs assured Defense Secretary Louis Johnson that Soviet nuclear activity was of the "highest priority."[93] Truman's second DCI, Hoyt Vandenberg, now air force chief of staff, was made responsible for long-range detection worldwide—something the United States had been studying since deploying nuclear weapons against Japan. In 1947 Hillenkoetter had estimated that it would take two years to complete a long-range monitoring system, although Bush's experts thought the DCI was too optimistic because reliable technology simply didn't yet exist.[94] As late as mid-1948, results of attempts to detect American tests on Eniwetok atoll in the South Pacific were generally "poor or worse."[95] Lacking detailed intelligence, the CIA and other agencies had predicted that a Soviet bomb was likely several years away when radiation "signatures" from the first Russian test, undertaken on August 29, were first detected over Alaska in September 1949.[96] Initially, both Secretary of Defense Johnson and NSC Executive Secretary Souers thought the radiation came from a Russian nuclear reactor accident rather than a bomb, and it was almost a month before Truman announced the Russian bomb on September 23, 1949.[97] Hillenkoetter told Congress that CIA analysts didn't have enough human or technical intelligence to allow accurate assessments, with Atomic Energy Commission Chairman David

Lilienthal adding, "In my opinion, our sources of information about Russian progress are so poor as to be merely arbitrary assumptions."[98] Indeed, it wasn't until 1956, six years after Hillenkoetter returned to the navy, that the CIA U-2 strategic reconnaissance aircraft was able to provide authoritative intelligence on Soviet nuclear and strategic weapons programs. The Soviet nuclear program was, in practical terms, impossible to penetrate in the late 1940s, and Hillenkoetter could only accept that his agency had failed to predict exactly when the Soviets would first detonate a bomb.

Two events in 1950 gave further evidence of Hillenkoetter's character—and of the difficult challenges facing his new organization. In one case, Hillenkoetter was almost alone in Washington in standing up for his staff, just as he had alone confronted general community attitudes in January 1946 in defending his black sailor against pervasive racial animosity. In February 1950 demagogic Republican Wisconsin senator Joseph McCarthy accused the State Department of harboring scores of communists—and the CIA of having one Red. In fact, as we now know from VENONA and from British historian Christopher Andrew's research on KGB archives, the Soviets had indeed been remarkably successful in penetrating American institutions, including the OSS and Department of State.[99] McCarthy did not have any facts to back up his reckless accusations, however, and the army was just beginning to analyze the KGB VENONA material. But for the next several years, McCarthy and his Red-baiting allies terrorized Washington, until his drunkenness and wild excess finally destroyed him. Only Hillenkoetter and the CIA resisted his initial attack. The DCI immediately sent McCarthy a detailed letter describing the careful security investigation made by both the OSS and CIA of the accused individual, and threatened to publicize the letter unless McCarthy stopped attacking the CIA. McCarthy agreed to do so if the DCI "did not make his letter public or make [the matter a] political issue." As a scholar said in 2005, "The CIA's first director has never been properly credited with standing up to Joe McCarthy."[100]

Thereafter the CIA was not damaged by the "Red Scare," but McCarthy did turn on the agency again, in what was called the "Lavender Scare," attacking homosexuals. And in this instance he was absolutely correct, for Hillenkoetter's old Paris colleague Carmel Offie was indeed openly and promiscuously homosexual.[101] Ironically, Offie was not really working directly for Hillenkoetter but for Kennan and Wisner's quasi-independent Office of Policy Coordination. Nonetheless, Hillenkoetter stepped forward to defend him in an extraordinary secret congressional hearing in July 1950, at which the DCI acknowledged Offie's homosexuality but made the blunt case that the CIA might need to use homosexuals in field operations, much as the Soviets used sexual entrapment to blackmail victims into spying. Hillenkoetter told the squeamish members that he was confident "no member . . . of the Congress would balk against our use of any technique to penetrate [Soviet] operations. . . . After all, intelligence is, at best, an extremely dirty business." Congress did not wish to hear anything further of such matters, and Wisner was able to keep Offie working for him under a contract rather than as a State Department or CIA officer.[102] Hillenkoetter also put himself on record in a personal letter to Offie on May 17, 1950, expressing "great reluctance" at receiving his formal resignation from the CIA and thanking him for his "very loyal and competent service . . . and for . . . the industry and skill you have at all times displayed in furthering the objectives of this organization."[103]

By then, however, DCI Hillenkoetter had already suffered two fatal wounds. The most immediate one was inflicted by Joseph Stalin when he gave his North Korean ally, Kim Il-Sung, Soviet blessing to attack South Korea, which Kim's forces did on June 25, 1950. The US government had thought the Soviets were more likely to engineer crises in Berlin, Greece, Turkey, or Iran, but through the spring of 1950, the CIA had been reporting on a steady concentration of North Korean military forces and on increasing North Korean guerrilla raids into the South. As Truman remembered: "Throughout the Spring the Central Intelligence reports said that the North Koreans might at any time decide to change from isolated raids to full-scale attack . . . but there was no information to give any clue as to whether an attack was certain or when it was likely to come. But [the CIA told me repeatedly] that there were any number of other spots in the world where the Russians 'possessed the capability' to attack."[104]

The Soviets had been training and equipping the North Koreans since 1946, but it was extremely difficult for the CIA to see into the hermit kingdom to estimate the strength or organization of the North Korean army. Many Europeans saw the North Korean attack as a prelude to a Soviet attack on West Germany, and although that did not seem plausible in those grim days, CIA senior officer David Murphy later called Stalin's approval of Kim's attack a "massive miscalculation." Stalin "failed to calculate the effect of the invasion on Western Europe and the United States" and foresee the Western decision to expand NATO and integrate the new German military into a common European defense.[105] The Korean attack also reversed the congressional tendency to cut the defense budget, and Congress quickly added $28 billion for defense. The draft was re-activated, and the US Army was increased to eighteen divisions, with four divisions going to Europe in 1951.[106] Despite crises in other parts of the world over the next few decades, the American military would maintain a strong defensive presence in West Germany until German re-unification and Saddam Hussein's attack on Kuwait in 1990. Only after the final disintegration of the Soviet Union in December

1991 would the American military forces—which arrived with the Second "Hell on Wheels" Armored Division in July 1945—finally be withdrawn from a free and united Berlin.

The day after the initial North Korean attack, both Secretary of State Acheson and Secretary of Defense Johnson told the Senate that the invasion of South Korea had been a "complete surprise." Despite what a historian called Acheson's "nimble trashing" of the CIA, he told Hillenkoetter that he had tried to pacify the Senate Appropriations Committee.[107] In the words of his legislative counsel Pforzheimer, "Hilly was furious" when he discovered that State and Defense had blamed his analysts for not warning of the attack, and he got Truman's permission to testify for the CIA, just as he had during the Bogota scandal. As he had done in the 1948 Bogota investigation, he brought CIA reports to the Hill and read the warnings to the senators. Hillenkoetter argued that while the CIA could not be expected to be able to predict the exact date of the North Korean attack—any more than OSS or military intelligence had been able to predict the exact date of the Pearl Harbor attack—the CIA had given policymakers, including Acheson, Johnson, and President Truman, adequate warning.[108] Most senators agreed, with California Republican William Knowland concluding, "The Central Intelligence Agency was doing its part of the job."

In part, Republicans' sympathy for Hillenkoetter can be explained by their hostility toward the State Department—and especially toward the patrician and self-assured Acheson—and also by a general desire to criticize the Truman administration by using CIA testimony on North Korea as further grounds for attack. Acheson returned their hostility, a feeling that senators doubtless sensed. Years later, in an oral interview for the Truman Presidential Library, Acheson vented: "I say Congress is too damn representative. It's just as stupid as the people are; just as uneducated, just as dumb, just as selfish."[109] Kennan expressed similar views in his memoirs: "I could not accept the assumption that Senators were all such idiots that they deserved admiring applause every time they could be persuaded . . . to do something sensible."[110]

For Sidney Souers and Harry Truman, the North Korean surprise was the final nail in DCI Hillenkoetter's coffin, but he had already suffered serious wounds from Allen Dulles more than a year earlier. Dulles, based upon his highly respected Bern OSS service, had hoped to replace Donovan as national intelligence chief and then, two years later, had expected to become Republican Thomas Dewey's Director of Central Intelligence (had Dewey defeated Truman in the 1948 election). Given his close political ties to Dewey, and his role in Dewey's criticisms of the CIA and Truman's international policy in general, it's remarkable that in early 1948 the Truman administration made Dulles the chairman of a committee investigating CIA operations and effectiveness. As Souers later explained the background, once he became executive secretary of the NSC in 1947, he casually reminded Secretary of Defense Forrestal that the NSC was supposed to supervise the CIA. Souers noted that at that point, Hillenkoetter had been DCI for only a few months, and the statutory CIA was even newer. There were no indications of trouble, and Souers considered the reminder completely innocent. Forrestal said he was too busy with the Defense Department, where the navy and air force were fighting bitterly for survival or dominance, and said the NSC executive secretary should take on the task. Souers responded that "if he wanted to supervise the CIA, he would still be DCI" and thus Forrestal chose a three-man survey group to produce a report. Years later, Souers said he would not have selected Dulles to lead the survey because of his connection to "arrogant and arbitrary" OSS director Donovan and his activities "coaching Dewey to attack CIA." Dulles and fellow survey group member William H. Jackson—who, as an Army Intelligence colonel, had served as Brigadier General Edwin Sibert's deputy when he was directing Operation RUSTY to use the Gehlen Org—were "certainly not the disinterested and impartial investigators that they were supposed to be." In Souers's words, they were both prejudiced against Hillenkoetter before they began their survey. In turn, Hillenkoetter thought the Dulles report was a "hatchet job" to destroy him and replace him as DCI.[111]

Remarkably, given that Souers himself had been director during the first disorganized and stressful months after the creation of the weak Central Intelligence Group—and was now executive secretary director of the NSC, with a very negative view of Allen Dulles—his admission that "they did not anticipate such a devastating report" is surprising. The survey acknowledged that "an efficient intelligence organization cannot be built overnight. It will require years of patient work to . . . do the job."[112] It also acknowledged great risks facing the United States: "[The possibility of] sudden and possibly devastating attack" from "a vast area of the world . . . behind an iron curtain where the normal sources of information are partially or wholly lacking," aided by "the far-flung activities of the [Red] fifth column, both here and abroad."[113] In such circumstances, conditions for intelligence collection were "uniquely difficult."[114] Clearly, without sufficient and accurate secret intelligence reporting, analysis and estimating were equally difficult. In summary, though, Dulles focused on Hillenkoetter:

It is the Director who must guide the organization . . . and win the confidence of . . . the Government. This is not an easy task. The Central Intelligence Agency has a diversified and difficult mission to perform. . . . Its success depends, to a large extent, on the support it receives from other agencies which may be ignorant of its problems and suspicious of its [authorities.] . . . the pressure to build rapidly has been strong and there has been little time in which to demonstrate substantial accomplishments.[115]

Even so, in a very legalistic sense, the CIA had indeed been given authorities and the DCI had been given responsibilities, particularly to coordinate the efforts of all US intelligence agencies and to produce National Intelligence Estimates to inform the NSC and the president, and help them develop well-reasoned national policy. In the single most pointed sentence in the whole report, the survey group concluded, "Since it is the task of the Director to see that the Agency carries out its assigned functions, the failure to do so is necessarily a reflection of inadequacies of direction."[116] In their view, the buck stopped with Hillenkoetter. Christopher Andrew, probably the most knowledgeable expert on the relations between American presidents and their intelligence chiefs, took another perspective:

The "inadequacies of direction" however were as much Truman's as Hillenkoetter's. Hilly was heavily outgunned on the NSC by the secretaries of both state and defense. Without the strong support of the president, he could not hope to fulfill the task . . . required of the DCI.[117]

Ludwell Montague, an early senior CIA analyst and historian, illustrated Hillenkoetter's problem and Truman's neglect with a small but telling anecdote: As a new two-star rear admiral, a rank he held during his entire term as director, Hilly was junior to every single military officer he was supposed to supervise, and much junior to the secretaries with whom he worked. His successor, Beetle Smith, came to the CIA as a three-star lieutenant general fresh from long service as chief of staff to Supreme Allied Commander Dwight Eisenhower and as ambassador to Moscow. Within a year, Truman refused to promote any other generals until Bradley reluctantly gave Smith his fourth star, making him the equal of all the service chiefs of staff, and greatly senior to every military intelligence chief. Perhaps Truman had learned from what Montague called Hillenkoetter's "painfully frustrating and thankless experience."[118]

It should also be noted that every DCI before or since has struggled to some degree to meet the standard laid out by Dulles and his partners. In 2005, concluding that DCIs could not, in fact, successfully accomplish the ideals of the National Security Act of 1947, the US Congress took both coordinating and estimating functions away from Director of Central Intelligence Porter Goss and gave them to a new official outside and above the Central Intelligence Agency: the new Director of National Intelligence.

Stung though he was by what he considered unreasonable and unfair criticism, which he felt underestimated the amount of resistance and hostility he had routinely faced from State and the military services, Hillenkoetter still made efforts to respond to some constructive suggestions. He had never been happy that Covert Action activities under Wisner were isolated from and independent of his chief of secret operations and agreed with the Dulles recommendation that OSO and OPC be combined. Naturally, the State Department resisted, with the Deputy Special Assistant for Intelligence Fisher Howe writing his chief, "It is obviously impossible to get a man big enough to be over Wisner and small enough to be under Hilly." Howe added, with obvious regret, that there was no hope Hillenkoetter would resign over the State Department's support for Wisner.[119]

The challenge of estimating was even more difficult, especially until the invention of remarkable technological systems like the U-2 strategic reconnaissance aircraft by the CIA in the mid-1950s. Only then, in the words of a CIA memo:

> For the first time we are really able to say that we have an understanding of much that was going on in the Soviet Union. We are no longer dependent on an "estimate" or a "judgment" or an "assessment". . . . [The U-2 has] already proven that many of our guesses on important subjects can be seriously wrong, that the estimates which form the basis for national policy can be projections from wrong guesses, and that as a consequence, our policy can indeed be bankrupt.[120]

On issues not subject to American technological superiority, unfortunately, analysis has never gotten easier and is still prey to uncertainty and what Sherman Kent called "the unknowable."[121]

Transferring the Flag

With characteristic bluntness, Souers considered Allen Dulles to be both biased and partisan in his criticism of the CIA but speaking years later concluded: "The fact remained that Hillenkoetter was a disaster as DCI. He was not qualified . . . and should never have been appointed." To Souers, himself of German descent, Hilly was an "amiable Dutchman." Since Hillenkoetter refused to resign to please the State Department's Fisher Howe, once the Korean War broke out, Souers told Truman it was "imperative" to replace him. Hillenkoetter himself also asked to return to sea duty after more than three thankless years as DCI.[122] As a successor, Truman suggested Walter Bedell Smith, based on his good performance as ambassador to Moscow, knowledge of the Soviet Union, and acceptability to both the Departments of State and Defense.[123] This appointment bitterly disappointed Dulles, who had argued strongly in his survey report for the benefits of long-term civilian leadership and the disadvantages of having military leaders, for whom the CIA was simply a temporary tour of duty.

Hillenkoetter returned to the navy with a tribute in the *Congressional Record* from John McCormack, who noted that he had served during the CIA's

> most difficult years . . . [in their criticisms of the CIA] people have tended to lose sight of the immense difficulties in building America's first permanent intelligence organization in the short period of three years. . . . It has fallen upon the admiral's shoulders to build an American system which is second to none. Those of us who have known of the development of the Central Intelligence Agency under his regime realize the strides that have been made and the credit that is due to Admiral Hillenkoetter for his great contribution to national security.[124]

A letter from Truman noted the president's

> heartfelt appreciation of the splendid service you have rendered as Director. . . . The work you did in developing this agency into an effective foreign intelligence service for the President . . . is worthy of highest praise. . . . With foresight, tenacity, and discretion you performed manifold duties in a manner designed to serve the national interest rather than that of any particular group.[125]

In turn, in a letter in early October, Hillenkoetter expressed his "sincere appreciation and gratitude for the understanding, consideration, and support you have always so generously and so cheerfully given me."[126] The internal White House description of his service noted his "extreme modesty and self-effacing devotion to duty; friendliness and good will in dealing with [colleagues]; patience and forbearance in the face of difficult but unavoidable problems arising from his task of coordinating the national intelligence effort."[127] Whatever else Hillenkoetter might have been, his successor was not patient, self-effacing, or friendly.

Beetle Smith, born in Indianapolis, Indiana, had started as a private in the Indiana National Guard and advanced to the rank of lieutenant general and the position of chief of staff for Supreme Allied Commander Dwight Eisenhower. After the war, Truman appointed Smith ambassador to Moscow, where he served for two and a half years, until Christmas 1948. Suffering from ulcers and unable to eat a normal diet, Smith was said to have an even temper: He was always angry. He told Eisenhower, "I wanted to avoid the intelligence job if possible, but . . . in light of the Korean affair, I did not feel I could refuse." He confided to a friend: "I expect the worst and am sure I won't be disappointed."[128] He was nominated as DCI in August 1950 and, with Hillenkoetter present, addressed the senators about "some of Hillenkoetter's troubles."

Walter Bedell Smith and Roscoe Hillenkoetter passing the torch, October 1950 (Courtesy of the CIA).

Incoming CIA Director Lieutenant General Walter Bedell Smith and outgoing Director Rear Admiral Hillenkoetter with CIA leadership—including general counsel Lawrence Houston (*between Smith and Hillenkoetter*), legislative counsel Walter Pforzheimer (*second from right*), and Office of Policy Coordination chief Frank Wisner (*far right*)—October 1950 (Courtesy of the CIA).

"There are only two personalities that I know of [to be DCI.] One is God, and the other is Stalin, and I do not know if even God can do it, because I do not know whether he is close enough in touch with Uncle Joe to know what he is talking about."[129] According to *Time* magazine, he added: "[The American people] expect you to be able to say that a war will start next Tuesday at 5:32 pm."[130]

Smith was accepted enthusiastically and unanimously by Congress, to whom he was "deferential, responsive, and soldierly." In World War II he had been known as Ike's hatchet man, and after his experience dealing with Allied intrigues and Stalin's paranoia, he was a tough, no-nonsense, highly skilled bureaucratic infighter. Smith, not completely candidly, told Souers that he knew nothing about intelligence and needed a deputy who did.[131] Not liking Dulles, Souers suggested his survey partner, William Jackson. The latter met with Smith and told him he had no intention of being "bawled out by a tyrannical soldier." Laughing and saying his bark was worse than his bite, Smith agreed to "no bawlings out."[132] Both Jackson and Smith understood that they needed to address the Dulles Commission recommendations and quickly brought back William Langer and Sherman Kent to create a real Office of National Estimates. Jackson urged Smith to bring in Allen Dulles as director of operations, and after Souers arranged a personal meeting between Dulles and Truman, the president agreed to the appointment.[133] Dulles brought Wisner's OPC back under CIA control, with the Office of Secret Operations and the Office of Policy Coordination being combined in August 1952 into a real Clandestine Service, called the Directorate of Plans to try to hide its espionage and Covert Action missions.[134] Neither Souers nor Smith ever warmed to Allen Dulles, and when President Eisenhower, in 1954, insisted Smith become John Foster Dulles's undersecretary of state, with Allen Dulles succeeding him as DCI, Souers grumbled that "there was a good deal [of] impropriety in appointing a brother of the Secretary of State to be DCI."[135]

Whatever Truman might have said publicly about "cloak and dagger" espionage and Covert Action, there is no question that he was willing to direct the CIA to use both. He was also a supporter of the communications intelligence (COMINT) methods that had made World War II MAGIC and ULTRA such powerful tools. Indeed, just as he was disbanding Donovan's OSS in September 1945, he approved continued US-British cooperation on communications and signals interception and decryption. The Army Security Agency, which proved so successful with Soviet VENONA messages, was created at the same time.[136] With the Korean War, DCI Smith demanded that the CIA finally be given access to this communications intelligence, and he got Truman to support a reorganization and consolidation of all military COMINT. Finally, almost eleven years after Pearl Harbor, President Truman, using a secret presidential memorandum, created a National Security Agency, which officially came into existence on November 4, 1952, the day Republican Dwight Eisenhower was elected president.

By then Rear Admiral Roscoe Hillenkoetter had again served in a hot war. Returning to the Fleet as Commander of Cruiser Division One of the Far East Seventh Fleet, his cruisers and the rest of the navy supported General of the Army Douglas MacArthur's American and UN soldiers fighting in Korea. In late 1950 the Chinese Communist People's Liberation Army entered the war and pushed surprised and outnumbered UN forces southward through the frozen North Korean mountains. Hillenkoetter, in his flagship *St. Paul*, commanded a gunfire support group of cruisers, destroyers, and rocket ships, creating a "ring of fire" around the port of Hungnam, and allowing some hundred thousand US and Korean soldiers—and almost as many Korean civilians—to escape in December 1950.

Rear Admiral Roscoe Hillenkoetter's flagship, *St. Paul*, covering the American withdrawal from Hungnam, Korea, December 1950 (Naval History and Heritage Command, 80-G-427198).

Hillenkoetter's warships were even joined by his old battleship command *Missouri* two days before Christmas 1950, as the Chinese wisely stayed out of range while the US soldiers and marines and Korean civilians were rescued from Hungnam by the US Navy.[137]

In 1956 Hillenkoetter, by now a vice admiral, was appointed inspector general of the navy and served as such until he retired in May 1957. Thereafter, he joined the management of the American Banner steamship line and, aside from

Korean refugees at Hungnam, December 1950 (National Archives College Park, "War and Conflict" album, photo 1479).

letters or interviews with historians curious about his role in the great events of World War II and the early Cold War, had only one more public association with intelligence issues.[138] This occasion was, however, truly extraordinary and has dominated general public knowledge of this now little-known and obscure man. On February 28, 1960, the *New York Times* reported that the US Air Force was warning its commands to treat UFO sightings as "serious business." Hillenkoetter, identified as a member of a privately funded National Investigations Committee on Aerial Phenomena, or NICAP, was quoted as saying, "It is time for the truth to be brought out in open Congressional Hearings." "Behind the scenes, high-ranking Air Force officers are soberly concerned about the UFOs but through secrecy and ridicule, many citizens are led to believe the unknown flying objects are nonsense." Hillenkoetter charged, "To hide the facts, the Air Force has silenced its personnel."[139]

This article caused some dismay within the CIA, for the Agency and the air force were indeed hiding facts that would become known worldwide two months later, when Gary Francis Powers, piloting a CIA U-2, was shot down over the Soviet Union on May 1, 1960. According to a chief historian of the National

Reconnaissance Office, and later of the CIA, highly secret U-2s on training missions were being spotted over the United States by civilian and military pilots. Mistaken for "unidentified flying objects," since no known airplane could fly so high, the CIA and air force created Project Blue Book, supposedly to record and track UFOs. In fact, the purpose of Blue Book was to convince people that they had not, in fact, seen a secret American spy plane. Obviously, Allen Dulles, by then DCI, had not shared knowledge of the U-2 program with his predecessor. The air force and CIA debated whether CIA general counsel Lawrence Houston, who had served as Hillenkoetter's Agency lawyer, should talk to the former director. Whether or not Houston had a quiet word with him, Hillenkoetter resigned from NICAP in 1962.[140] This has not prevented the first CIA director from being widely known today primarily among UFO conspiracy theorists, although now the U-2 is equally widely known. Hillenkoetter died on June 18, 1982, at the age of eighty-five in Weehawken, New Jersey, where he and his wife had lived since his retirement from the navy. In his obituary, the *New York Times* quoted Navy Chaplain Captain Joshua Goldberg as calling the admiral "a symbol of what an American should be." "He was modest, and people who served under him just loved him."[141] He and his wife are buried at Arlington National Cemetery, immediately across the Potomac River from his office at the old OSS and CIA headquarters on a hill just above the Lincoln Memorial in Foggy Bottom, Washington, DC.

Sidney Souers also returned to business life, although he and his wife remained close to the President he addressed as "Boss." Three years after Hillenkoetter's suspicions about UFOs attracted the attention of the *New York Times*, Truman himself caused a great stir in late December 1963 by complaining that the CIA had become "an operational and at times a policy-making arm" "injected into peacetime cloak and dagger operations" far outside the "original assignment" "as the intelligence arm of the President."[142] In Truman's view, the CIA "is being interpreted as a symbol of sinister and mysterious foreign intrigue." Souers quickly wrote Truman a "Dear Boss" letter, enthusiastically agreeing and blaming Allen Dulles, who "caused the CIA to wander too far from the original goal established by you." "Its principal effort [seems] to cause revolutions in smaller countries around the globe."

Truman's criticism stunned the CIA because "with his explicit but secret approval . . . CIA covert action . . . were initiated to help contain the communist threat."[143] Allen Dulles was also deeply upset, even though he had been fired as DCI two years earlier by President John F. Kennedy, after the spectacular failure of the CIA Bay of Pigs covert action effort to overthrow Cuban leader Fidel

Castro in April 1961. Dulles immediately wrote back to Truman to remind the president that

> you also were first to take stock of the fact that the communist subversive threat could not be met solely by the overt type of assistance. . . . I can say—frankly—that I feel there are parts of your article . . . which might be interpreted as a repudiation of a policy which you had the great courage and wisdom to initiate 15 years ago.[144]

A few months later, in April 1964, clearly still smarting from the criticism, Dulles went to visit Truman at his presidential library office in Independence, Missouri. As David McCullough quoted Dean Acheson: "Truman might be fierce and hot-tempered in writing but was always very considerate of people's feelings in person."[145] He was now hospitable and considerate with Eisenhower's DCI. In a memo he wrote after the meeting, Dulles said he reminded Truman of the "procedures . . . by CIA to meet the creeping subversion of communism. . . . I reviewed the various steps which had been taken under [your] authority . . . of the problems we had faced during the Italian elections of 1948. . . . Mr. Truman . . . interjected reminiscences of his own, recalled vividly the whole Italian election problem. . . . At no time did Mr. Truman express other than complete agreement with the viewpoint I expressed."[146]

It was clear that both Truman and Souers felt a deep pride in and affection for the Central Intelligence Agency they had created—even if they did choose either to forget or gloss over some of the aspects of what DCI Hillenkoetter had told Congress was "at best, an extremely dirty business" while he was trying to save Carmel Offie from Joe McCarthy's venom.[147] In a letter to a friend in October 1949, Souers said he had "gotten a great kick out of helping these babies [the NSC and CIA] begin to walk." Upon leaving Washington at the end of 1952, he told the same friend, "I am at last getting away for good with the feeling that both the National Security Council and the Central Intelligence Agency are pretty solidly fitted into the government machinery."[148] In a letter dated January 17, 1953, Truman told Souers, "No President ever had a more trustworthy, loyal and capable associate."[149]

Twenty years later, on January 14, 1973, Souers died in Saint Louis. Two days later, Richard Helms, who had served in the OSS and was now DCI, wrote his widow:

> I wish to commemorate the great contribution he made to our country in the development of the concept of central intelligence after World War

II . . . from these events came . . . the National Security Council and the Central Intelligence Agency, enabling our Government to meet its critical intelligence needs through the most turbulent times of the cold war. . . . We who inherited your husband's concept are particularly aware of what our country owes him in the field of national security.[150]

The last word on Truman's CIA belongs to the man himself. On the wall of the main corridor—on the first floor of the CIA Building that Allen Dulles built in bucolic Langley, Virginia, overlooking a peaceful interior courtyard—hangs a row of presidential portraits, beginning with the Man from Missouri. In his own hand, Truman wrote, "To the Central Intelligence Agency, a necessity to the President of the United States, from one who knows."[151]

Harry S. Truman's inscription to the CIA (Courtesy of the CIA).

Notes

Introduction

1. Thomas Troy, "Truman on CIA," *Studies in Intelligence* 20, no. 1 (Spring 1976): 21.

2. Joseph C. Goulden, *The Best Years: 1945–50* (New York: Atheneum, 1976), 213.

Chapter One

1. Wyman H. Packard, *A Century of U.S. Naval Intelligence* (Washington, DC: Department of the Navy, 1996), 2.

2. Ibid.

3. Ibid., 3.

4. Richard E. Schroeder, *Missouri at Sea: Warships with Show-Me State Names* (Columbia: University of Missouri Press, 2004), 55–57.

5. Ibid., 63–64.

6. Christopher Andrew, *For the President's Eyes Only: Secret Intelligence and the American Presidency from Washington to Bush* (New York: Harper Perennial, 1996), 30.

7. Ibid., 31.

8. Ibid., 42.

9. Ibid., 33–34.

10. Ibid., 35.

11. Ibid., 39.

12. Packard, *Century of U.S. Naval Intelligence*, 12–13, 248.

13. Ibid., 63.

14. Patrick Devenny, "Captain John A. Gade, U.S. Navy: An Early Advocate of Central Intelligence," *Studies in Intelligence* 56, no. 3 (2012): 22–23.

Studies in Intelligence is a publication of the CIA. Please note that citations of volume, number, and page number for this publication are not consistent from issue to issue.

15. Ibid., 23–24.

16. Ibid., 27.

17. John A. Gade, *All My Born Days: Experiences of a Naval Intelligence Officer in Europe* (New York: Charles Scribner's Sons, 1942), 225.

18. *Gould's St. Louis Directory for 1917* (St. Louis: Gould Directory Co., 1917), 1025, http://dl.mospace.umsystem.edu/umsl/islandora/object/umsl%3A166303#page /1013/mode/1up.

19. *Rear Admiral Roscoe H. Hillenkoetter Biography*, US Navy Bureau of Personnel, May 27, 1947.

20. *Vice Admiral Roscoe H. Hillenkoetter Biography*, Naval Historical Center, Biographies Branch, 1–450, May 16, 1957.

21. *Pennsylvania, Philadelphia Marriage Indexes, 1885–1951*, Family Search, December 7, 2014, https://familysearch.org/ark:/61903/1:1:JJBS-J6N, citing license number 630128, Clerk of the Orphan's Court, City Hall; and *New York, New York Passenger and Crew Lists, 1909, 1925–1957*, Family Search, October 2, 2015, https:/ /familysearch.org/ark:/61903/1:1:24VK-BQD, citing *Immigration, New York, New York, United States*, National Archives Microfilm Publication T715. The *SS Washington* arrived at New York on September 20, 1935.

22. Jeffrey M. Dorwart, *Conflict of Duty: The U.S. Navy's Intelligence Dilemma, 1919–1945* (Annapolis, MD: Naval Institute Press, 1983), 63, 76.

23. *New York, New York Passenger and Crew Lists, 1909, 1925–1957*, Family Search, October 3, 2015, https://familysearch.org/ark:/61903/1:1:24PD-ZSX, citing *Immigration, New York City, New York, United States*, National Archives Microfilm Publication T715. Jane C. Hillenkoetter arrived in New York on the *SS America* on April 4, 1947.

24. Will Brownell and Richard N. Billings, *So Close to Greatness: A Biography of William C. Bullitt* (New York: Macmillan, 1987), 204.

25. David Alvarez and Eduard Mark, *Spying through a Glass Darkly: American Espionage against the Soviet Union, 1945–1946* (Lawrence: University Press of Kansas, 2016), 2.

26. Ibid., 2–3.

27. Douglas MacArthur II, oral interview, December 15, 1986, Library of Congress, http://www.loc.gov/item/mfdipbib000732.

28. Gade, *All My Born Days*, 294.

29. "Americans Reach France in Safety," *New York Times*, January 27, 1939.

30. Attaché's Report, February 3, 1939, Entry 98, Box 873, Register 22178-C, Records Group 38, National Archives and Records Administration, Office of Naval Intelligence (hereafter NARA ONI RG38).

31. Roscoe Hillenkoetter to Orville H. Bullitt, October 19, 1970, in *For the President: Personal and Secret; Correspondence Between Franklin D. Roosevelt and William C. Bullitt*, ed. Orville H. Bullitt (Boston: Houghton Mifflin, 1972), 357–58.

32. NARA ONI RG38, Entry 98, Box 1007, Register 22597, July 29, 1938.

33. NARA ONI RG38, Entry 98, Box 550, Register 15373-H, September 12, 1938.

34. Ibid., September 27, 1938.

35. NARA ONI RG38, Entry 98, Box 550, Register 1889-A, October 22, 1938.

36. NARA ONI RG38, Entry 98, Box 592, Register 15653-E, December 6, 1938.

37. NARA ONI RG38, Entry 98, Box 220, Register 16158-L, December 16, 1938.

38. Captain Ellis Stone, NARA ONI RG38, Entry 98, Box 550, Register 15373-H, July 18, 1939.

39. Packard, *A Century of U.S. Naval Intelligence*, 70.

40. Captain John Gade, Brussels, NARA ONI RG38, Entry 98, Box 857, Register 22839-A, December 28, 1939.

41. Robert Daniel Murphy, *Diplomat among Warriors* (New York: Doubleday, 1964), 35–36.

42. *Rear Admiral Roscoe H. Hillenkoetter Biography* (see chap. 1, n. 19).

43. Clare Boothe, "Europe in the Spring: An American Playwright Reports on a Continent's Last Days of Freedom," *Life*, July 29, 1940, 75; and Kim M. Juntunen, "US Army Attachés and the Spanish Civil War, 1936–1939: The Gathering of Technical and Tactical Intelligence" (master's thesis, United States Military Academy, 1990).

44. Murphy, *Diplomat among Warriors*, 35–36.

45. Richard Harris Smith, *OSS: The Secret History of America's First Central Intelligence Agency* (Guilford, CT: Lyons Press, 2005), 178–80.

46. Murphy, *Diplomat among Warriors*, 42–44.

47. Bullitt, *For the President*, 469–70; and Boothe, "Europe in the Spring."

48. Murphy, *Diplomat among Warriors*, 45.

49. Brownell and Billings, *So Close to Greatness*, 262.

50. Murphy, *Diplomat among Warriors*, 62–63.

51. NARA ONI RG38, C-9-e, Box 439, Register 19447, September 4, 1940, National Archives College Park (hereafter NACP).

52. NARA ONI RG38, C-9-e, Box 147, Register 19447c, September 5, 1940, NACP.

53. "Nazis Halt US Mail," *New York Times*, August 1, 1940; and "US Mail Gets to Paris," *New York Times*, August 4, 1940.

54. Murphy, *Diplomat among Warriors*, 66–70.

55. NARA ONI RG38, Entry 98, Box 220, Register 18889-A, September 11, 1940.

56. Fleet Admiral William D. Leahy, *I Was There: The Personal Story of the Chief of Staff to Presidents Roosevelt and Truman Based on His Notes and Diaries Made at the Time* (New York: McGraw-Hill, 1950), 10–13; and Smith, *OSS*, 55.

57. NARA ONI RG38, C-9-e, Box 439, Register 19447, January 21, 1941, NACP.

58. Henry H. Adams, *Witness to Power: The Life of Fleet Admiral William D. Leahy* (Annapolis, MD: Naval Institute Press, 1985), 148.

59. *New York, New York Passenger and Crew Lists, 1909, 1925–1957*, Family Search, October 2, 2015, https://familysearch.org/ark:/61903/1:1:24LX-V34, citing *Immigration, New York, New York, United States*, National Archives Microfilm Publication T715, film 6578, digital folder 004879871, image 00818. Hillenkoetter flew on the Pan Am Yankee Clipper from Lisbon to New York, arriving on September 15, 1941.

60. Hillenkoetter to Douglas MacArthur, 5 June 1947, American Embassy Paris, C02130062, CIA files; and Eric Pace, "Douglas MacArthur 2nd, 88, Former Ambassador to Japan," *New York Times*, November 17, 1997.

61. Douglas MacArthur II, oral interview, January 29, 1987, Library of Congress, www.loc.gov/item/mfdipbib000732.

62. Raymond P. Brandt, "St. Louis Admiral Expected to Head U.S. Intelligence: May Get New Job," *St. Louis Post-Dispatch*, February 27, 1947.

63. NARA ONI RG38, C-9-e, Box 147, Register 19447-C, July 15, 1941, NACP.

64. Smith, *OSS*, 41.

65. John G. Norris, "A 'Maquis' Runs Our Central Intelligence: He's from the Missouri," *Washington Post*, May 4, 1947.

66. Leahy, *I Was There*, 29.

67. Ibid., 35.

68. Ibid., 21–22.

69. Arthur B. Darling, "The Birth of Central Intelligence," *Studies in Intelligence* 10, no. 2 (Spring 1966): 33.

70. Douglas MacArthur II, oral interview, March 31, 1987, Library of Congress, www.loc.gov/item/mfdipbib000732.

71. Murphy, *Diplomat among Warriors*, 91.

72. Ibid., 90–92.

73. Smith, *OSS*, 46.

74. *Hawaii, Honolulu Passenger Lists, 1900–1953*, Family Search, December 30, 2014, https://familysearch.org/ark:/61903/1:1:QV9Z-BP7N, citing ship, National Archives Microfilm Publication A3422, film number 234, digital folder 007501237, image 00055. The *SS Lurline* docked at Honolulu on November 14, 1941.

75. *Vice Admiral Roscoe H. Hillenkoetter Biography* (see chap. 1, n. 20).

Chapter Two

1. Andrew, *For the President's Eyes Only*, 68–69.

2. Thomas R. Johnson, *American Cryptology during the Cold War, 1945–1989: Book 1: The Struggle for Centralization, 1945–1960* (Fort Meade, MD: Center for Cryptologic History, National Security Agency, 1995), 1.

3. William Casey, *The Secret War against Hitler* (Washington, DC: Regnery Gateway, 1988), 7.

4. Memorandum to the commander in chief, Pacific Fleet, "The Senior Surviving Officer [RHH], USS West Virginia, 'Report of Action of December 7, 1941,'" December 11, 1941, Navy History Center, Washington, DC.

5. Packard, *Century of U.S. Naval Intelligence*, 19–21; and Mark Edward Harris, "A Family's Brush with Infamy," *Los Angeles Times Magazine*, May 13, 2001.

6. *Dictionary of American Naval Fighting Ships* (hereafter *DANFS*), s.v. "West Virginia" and "Maryland," April 22, 2017, https://www.history.navy.mil/research /histories/ship-histories/danfs.html; and *Vice Admiral Roscoe H. Hillenkoetter Biography*; and Ronald H. Spector, *Eagle against the Sun: The American War with Japan* (New York: Vintage Books, 1985), 175.

7. *Vice Admiral Roscoe H. Hillenkoetter Biography*.

8. Herbert O. Yardley, *The American Black Chamber* (New York: Ballantine Books, 1981), xi–xiii.

9. David Kahn, *The Codebreakers: The Story of Secret Writing* (New York: Macmillan, 1967), 8.

10. Spector, *Eagle against the Sun*, 101–8.

11. "MacArthur, Douglas," US Army Center of Military History, http://www .history.army.mil/moh/wwII-m-s.html#MacARTHUR.

12. Spector, *Eagle against the Sun*, 153–55.

13. Edwin T. Layton, Roger Pineau, and John Costello, *And I Was There: Pearl Harbor and Midway—Breaking the Secrets* (New York: William Morrow, 1985); and Jeffrey M. Moore, *Spies for Nimitz: Joint Military Intelligence in the Pacific War* (Annapolis, MD: Naval Institute Press, 2004), 5.

14. Layton, Pineau, and Costello, *I Was There*, 20–21.

15. Patrick D. Weadon, *The Battle of Midway: AF Is Short of Water* (Fort Meade, MD: National Security Agency, Center for Cryptologic History, 2000). https://www .nsa.gov/about/cryptologic-heritage/historical-figures-publications/publications/ wwii/battle-midway.shtml.

16. Layton, Pineau, and Costello, *I Was There*, 468; and Moore, *Spies for Nimitz*, 12.

17. Moore, *Spies for Nimitz*, 13; and *Vice Admiral Roscoe H. Hillenkoetter Biography*.

18. Spector, *Eagle against the Sun*, 13–20.

19. Kermit Roosevelt, ed., *War Report of the OSS (Office of Strategic Services)* (New York: Walker and Co., 1976), 2:365.

20. Spector, *Eagle against the Sun*, 189–90.

21. W. J. Holmes, *Doubled-Edged Secrets: U.S. Naval Intelligence Operations in the Pacific during World War II* (Annapolis, MD: Naval Institute Press, 1979), 122–23.

22. Ibid., 123.

23. Ibid., 124.

24. Ibid., 126–29.

25. Spector, *Eagle against the Sun*, 229–30.

26. Arthur B. Darling, "DCI Hillenkoetter: Soft Sell and Stick," *Studies in Intelligence* 13, no. 1 (Winter 1969): 33.

27. *DANFS*, s.v. "Dixie"; and *Vice Admiral Roscoe H. Hillenkoetter Biography*.

28. Moore, *Spies for Nimitz*, 237.

29. Packard, *Century of U.S. Naval Intelligence*, 216, 230–31.

Chapter Three

1. Joseph E. Persico, *Roosevelt's Secret War: FDR and World War II Espionage* (New York: Random House, 2001), xi–xii.

2. Andrew, *For the President's Eyes Only*, 82, 85.

3. Andrew, *For the President's Eyes Only*, 95; and Thomas F. Troy, *Donovan and the CIA: A History of the Establishment of the Central Intelligence Agency* (Frederick, MD: University Publications of America, 1981), 26–33.

4. Troy, *Donovan and the CIA*, 39.

5. Ibid., 42.

6. Ibid., 52.

7. Ibid., 417. Donovan to Knox, April 26, 1941.

8. Ibid., 57.

9. Ibid., 63.

10. Ibid., 423.

11. Smith, *OSS*, 17.

12. Roosevelt, *War Report of the OSS*, 1:19.

13. Troy, *Donovan and the CIA*, 131.

14. Ibid., 427.

15. Clark Clifford with Richard Holbrooke, *Counsel to the President: A Memoir* (New York: Random House, 1991), 165.

16. Roosevelt, *War Report of the OSS*, 1:16.

17. Smith, *OSS*, 26–31.

18. Stanley P. Lovell, *Of Spies and Stratagems* (Englewood Cliffs, NJ: Prentice Hall, 1963), 17.

19. Ibid., 22; and H. Keith Melton, *OSS Special Weapons and Equipment: Spy Devices of WW II* (New York: Sterling Publishing, 1992).

20. Lovell, *Of Spies and Stratagems*, 41.

21. Melton, *OSS Special Weapons and Equipment*, 83; and Lovell, *Of Spies and Stratagems,* 56.

22. Robin W. Winks, *Cloak and Gown, 1939–1961: Scholars in the Secret War* (New York: William Morrow, 1987), 67.

23. Roosevelt, *War Report of the OSS*, 1:167.

24. Winks, *Cloak and Gown*, 62, 71–72.

25. Ibid., 104.

26. Andrew, *For the President's Eyes Only*, 133.

27. Winks, *Cloak and Gown*, 76.

28. Ibid., 77.

29. Roosevelt, *War Report of the OSS*, 1:175.

30. Casey, *Secret War against Hitler*, 81.
31. Smith, *OSS*, 36.
32. Winks, *Cloak and Gown*, 84–85.
33. Smith, *OSS*, 46–58.
34. Ibid., 26, 31.
35. Richard E. Schroeder, "The Hitler Youth as a Paramilitary Organization" (PhD dissertation, University of Chicago, 1975), 1–7.
36. Smith, *OSS*, 144.
37. Ibid., 147.
38. Winks, *Cloak and Gown*, 190–91.
39. Roosevelt, *War Report of the OSS*, 2:viii.
40. Casey, *Secret War against Hitler*, 43–44.
41. Smith, *OSS*, 153.
42. Casey, *Secret War against Hitler*, 26.
43. Roosevelt, *War Report of the OSS*, 2:192–93.
44. Elizabeth P. McIntosh, *Sisterhood of Spies: The Women of the OSS* (New York: Dell, 1998), 147–59.
45. Smith, *OSS*, 158–65.
46. Ibid., 156.
47. Casey, *Secret War against Hitler*, 21.
48. Smith, *OSS*, 158.
49. Ibid., 169–70.
50. Roosevelt, *War Report of the OSS*, 2:ix.
51. Casey, *Secret War against Hitler*, 111–12.
52. Smith, *OSS*, 179.
53. Ibid., 177.
54. Casey, *Secret War against Hitler*, 146, 154.
55. Peter Grose, *Gentleman Spy: The Life of Allen Dulles* (London: Andre Deutsch, 1995), 111–16.
56. Ibid., 148.
57. Roosevelt, *War Report of the OSS*, 2:273.
58. Smith, *OSS*, 192–98.
59. Roosevelt, *War Report of the OSS*, 2:278–79.
60. Smith, *OSS*, 200–201.
61. J. C. Masterman, *The Double-Cross System in the War of 1939 to 1945* (New Haven: Yale University Press, 1972).
62. Winks, *Cloak and Gown*, 344.
63. Roosevelt, *War Report of the OSS*, 2:305–7.
64. Ibid., 287–89.
65. Winks, *Cloak and Gown*, 93.
66. Casey, *Secret War against Hitler*, 188–98.
67. Ibid., 201–4.

68. Smith, *OSS*, 212.

69. Roosevelt, *War Report of the OSS*, 1:273.

70. Smith, *OSS*, 216.

71. Ibid., 221.

72. Ibid., 219–20.

73. Roosevelt, *War Report of the OSS*, 1:2–3.

74. Smith, *OSS*, 223.

75. Ibid., 225–56.

76. Ibid., 265.

77. Smith, *OSS*, 229; and Michael Warner, *The Office of Strategic Services: America's First Intelligence Agency* (Washington, DC: Central Intelligence Agency, 2002), 18.

78. Roosevelt, *War Report of the OSS*, 2:384–85.

79. "Behind Enemy Lines in Burma: The Stuff of Intelligence Legend," ed. Troy J. Sacquety, *Studies in Intelligence*, no. 11 (Fall-Winter 2001); and Roosevelt, *War Report of the OSS*, 2:391.

80. Smith, *OSS*, 261.

81. Roosevelt, *War Report of the OSS*, 2:449.

82. Smith, *OSS*, 260.

83. Roosevelt, *War Report of the OSS*, 2:460.

84. Smith, *OSS*, 272.

85. Roosevelt, *War Report of the OSS*, 1:116.

86. Ibid., 2:408.

87. Ibid., 2:410.

88. Smith, *OSS*, 299–308.

89. Ibid., 309–18.

90. Ibid., 321–25.

91. Ibid., 258.

92. David F. Rudgers, *Creating the Secret State: The Origins of the Central Intelligence Agency, 1943–1947* (Lawrence: University of Kansas Press, 2000), 11–12.

93. Roosevelt, *War Report of the OSS*, 1:xi.

94. Rudgers, *Creating the Secret State*, 13.

95. Warner, *Office of Strategic Services*, 9.

96. Roosevelt, *War Report of the OSS*, 2:xvi.

Chapter Four

1. David McCullough, *Truman* (New York: Simon and Schuster, 1992), 320–21.

2. Merle Miller, *Plain Speaking: An Oral Biography of Harry S. Truman* (New York: Berkley Publishing, 1974), 26.

3. McCullough, *Truman*, 118.

4. Ibid., 185.

5. William Henhoeffer and James Hanrahan, "Souers Speaks Out: Notes on the Early DCIs," *Studies in Intelligence* 33, no. 1 (Spring 1989): 29.

6. McCullough, *Truman*, 231–33.

7. Ibid., 271.

8. Ibid., 259, 282, 288.

9. Ibid., 262.

10. Ibid., 286–87.

11. Ibid., 292.

12. Ibid., 327.

13. Robert J. Donovan, *Conflict and Crisis: The Presidency of Harry S. Truman, 1945–1948* (Columbia: University of Missouri Press, 1977), 17.

14. McCullough, *Truman*, 349–50; and Omar N. Bradley and Clay Blair, *A General's Life: An Autobiography by General of the Army Omar N. Bradley* (New York: Simon and Schuster, 1983), 429.

15. Adams, *Witness to Power*, 280.

16. Donovan, *Conflict and Crisis*, xv, 13.

17. Donovan, *Conflict and Crisis*, 12; and McCullough, *Truman*, 373.

18. McCullough, *Truman*, 372.

19. Adams, *Witness to Power*, 294; and McCullough, *Truman*, 393.

20. McCullough, *Truman*, 367.

21. Joel Achenbach, "70 Years Later, a Test in New Mexico Casts a Shadow," *Washington Post*, July 16, 2015.

22. Adams, *Witness to Power*, 289–90; and Douglas J. MacEachin, *The Final Months of the War with Japan: Signals Intelligence, U.S. Invasion Planning, and the A-Bomb Decision* (Washington, DC: Central Intelligence Agency, Center for the Study of Intelligence, 1998).

23. McCullough, *Truman*, 419.

24. Gary Kern, "How 'Uncle Joe' Bugged FDR," *Studies in Intelligence* 47, no. 1 (2003); and McCullough, *Truman*, 430–43.

25. Jeffrey T. Richelson, *Spying on the Bomb: American Nuclear Intelligence from Nazi Germany to Iran and North Korea* (New York: W. W. Norton, 2006), 67.

26. Christopher Andrew and Vasili Mitrokhin, *The Sword and the Shield: The Mitrokhin Archive and the Secret History of the KGB* (New York: Basic Books, 1999), 114–45; and Robert Louis Benson and Michael Warner, eds., *Venona: Soviet Espionage and the American Response, 1939–1957* (Washington, DC: National Security Agency and Central Intelligence Agency, 1996).

27. Bradley and Blair, *General's Life*, 441, 448.

28. Clifford with Holbrooke, *Counsel to the President*, 165.

29. Andrew, *For the President's Eyes Only*, 147; and Rudgers, *Creating the Secret State*, 25–31.

30. Rudgers, *Creating the Secret State*, 34, citing the April 27, 1945, *Washington Post*.

31. Andrew, *For the President's Eyes Only*, 56–57; and Rudgers, *Creating the Secret State*, 37.

32. Rudgers, *Creating the Secret State*, 38–39, 42; and Andrew, *For the President's Eyes Only*, 164.

33. Miller, *Plain Speaking*, 391.

34. Andrew, *For the President's Eyes Only*, 159.

35. Clifford with Holbrooke, *Counsel to the President*, 165; and Rudgers, *Creating the Secret State*, 45–46.

36. Rudgers, *Creating the Secret State*, 45–46.

37. Nicholas Dujmovic, "Drastic Actions Short of War: The Origins and Applications of CIA's Covert Paramilitary Function in the Early Cold War," *Journal of Military History* 76, no. 3 (July 2012): 781.

38. Rudgers, *Creating the Secret State*, 43.

39. Clifford with Holbrooke, *Counsel to the President*, 165.

40. Bradley and Blair, *General's Life*, 463.

41. Rudgers, *Creating the Secret State*, 74, 83.

42. Ibid., 54, 60–61.

43. Ibid., 74.

44. Henhoeffer and Hanrahan, "Souers Speaks Out."

45. Ted Schafers, "He Helped Make History: Rear Admiral Sidney W. Souers of St. Louis Played a Big Role in Shaping U.S. Policy Under Truman," *St. Louis Globe-Democrat*, October 9, 1966.

46. Rudgers, *Creating the Secret State*, 64.

47. *Rear Admiral Sidney W. Souers Biography*, Naval Historical Center, Biographies Branch, 01-023, December 17, 1952.

48. Schafers, "He Helped Make History."

49. NARA ONI RG38, Entry UD38, Interrogations 1941–45, Box 14, U-352, NACP.

50. Office of Naval Operations, Division of Naval Intelligence (ONI), *U-352 Sunk by U.S.C.G. Icarus 5-9-42, Serial No. 2, O.N.I. 250 Series* (Washington, DC: Government Printing Office, 1942), https://www.history.navy.mil/research/library/online-reading-room/title-list-alphabetically/u/u352-sunk-by-uscg-icarus.html.

51. NARA ONI RG38, U-352, NACP.

52. Henhoeffer and Hanrahan, "Souers Speaks Out."

53. David M. Barrett, *The CIA and Congress: The Untold Story from Truman to Kennedy* (Lawrence: University Press of Kansas, 2005), 18.

54. Andrew, *For the President's Eyes Only*, 164–66; and Darling, "Birth of Central Intelligence."

55. Harry S. Truman, *Years of Trial and Hope,* vol. 2 of *Memoirs by Harry S. Truman* (New York: Doubleday, 1956), 60.

56. Ibid., 58; and Henhoeffer and Hanrahan, "Souers Speaks Out."

57. Clifford with Holbrooke, *Counsel to the President*, 163, 167.

58. Sara L. Sale, "Admiral Sidney W. Souers and President Truman," *Missouri Historical Review* 86 (October 1991): 56.

59. McCullough, *Truman*, 78.

60. Adams, *Witness to Power*, 313–14.

61. Schroeder, *Missouri at Sea*, 109.

62. Clifford with Holbrooke, *Counsel to the President*, 100–101.

63. Ibid., 146–48.

64. Ibid., 165.

65. Ibid., 167.

66. Henhoeffer and Hanrahan, "Souers Speaks Out."

67. Captain D. D. Dupre to Captain William Heard, 6 April 1945, NARA ONI RG38, Entry UD3, Foreign Intelligence Branch, Correspondence with Naval Attachés 1930–48, Box 13, NACP.

68. Ibid.

69. NARA ONI RG38, Entry 98B, C-10-j, Box 174, Register 15373, April 3–16, 1945, NACP.

70. Eric Pace, "Douglas MacArthur 2nd"; and Douglas MacArthur II, oral interview, Library of Congress, www.loc.gov/item/mfdipbib000732.

71. Paris Activities July 1–December 31, 1947, NARA ONI RG38, Entry UD3, Correspondence with Attachés, Box 13, February 19, 1948, NACP.

72. Semi-Annual Report, July 1, 1946–March 28, 1947, NARA ONI RG38, UD3, Box 13, NACP.

73. Ibid.

74. Ibid.

75. Chief of Naval Intelligence (CNI) to Paris, September 8, 1947, NARA ONI RG38, Entry UD3, Box 13, NACP.

76. NARA ONI RG38, Entry UD3, Box 13, March 28, 1947, NACP.

77. Andrew, *For the President's Eyes Only*, 168–69; and Gary M. Breneman, "Lawrence R. Houston: A Biography," *Studies in Intelligence* 30, no. 1 (Spring 1986).

78. Clifford with Holbrooke, *Counsel to the President*, 168.

79. Andrew, *For the President's Eyes Only*, 169.

80. Arthur B. Darling, "With Vandenberg as DCI Part I: Some Functions Centralized," *Studies in Intelligence* 12, no. 3 (Summer 1968): 79; and Arthur B. Darling, "With Vandenberg as DCI Part II: Coordination in Practice," *Studies in Intelligence* 12, no. 4 (Fall 1968): 75.

81. Clifford with Holbrooke, *Counsel to the President*, 110–11, 123, 129.

82. Bradley and Blair, *General's Life*, 470–73.

83. Clifford with Holbrooke, *Counsel to the President*, 130–33.

84. Ibid., 143–47.

85. Ibid., 143.

86. Ibid., 169–70.

87. Barrett, *CIA and Congress*, 18.

88. "New Intelligence Chief Is Named; Gen. Vandenberg Returns to AAF; Admiral Hillenkoetter Is Third Director of Central Group," *New York Times*, May 2, 1947.

89. Clifford with Holbrooke, *Counsel to the President,* 156–58.

90. Bradley and Blair, *General's Life,* 470.

91. Clifford with Holbrooke, *Counsel to the President,* 16–22, 169.

92. Andrew, *For the President's Eyes Only,* 169; and *Rear Admiral Sidney W. Souers Biography.*

93. "Sidney W. Souers, Intelligence Aide, First Secretary of National Security Council, Is Dead," *New York Times,* January 16, 1973.

94. "Confidential Advisor," editorial, *Washington Post,* December 8, 1952.

95. Anthony Leviero, "Coordinator of Security: Sidney Souers Brings Wide Training to the Task of Advising the President on National Defense," *New York Times Magazine,* April 24, 1949.

96. Smith, *OSS,* 17; and Roosevelt, *War Report of the OSS,* 1:19.

97. United States Naval Academy, *Lucky Bag 1920* (Annapolis, MD, 1920), 168.

98. Darling, "DCI Hillenkoetter," 40.

99. Ibid., 42–43.

100. Ibid., 47.

101. Ibid., 54–55.

Chapter Five

1. James H. Critchfield, *Partners at the Creation: The Men Behind Postwar Germany's Defense and Intelligence Establishments* (Annapolis, MD: Naval Institute Press, 2003), 67.

2. David E. Murphy, Sergei A. Kondrashev, and George Bailey, *Battleground Berlin: CIA vs KGB in the Cold War* (New Haven: Yale University Press, 1997), xxiv–xxv.

3. Smith, *OSS,* 221.

4. Critchfield, *Partners at the Creation,* 11.

5. Keith Lowe, *Savage Continent: Europe in the Aftermath of World War II* (New York: St. Martin's Press, 2012), 24.

6. Critchfield, *Partners at the Creation,* 13–15.

7. Ibid., 148; and Bradley and Blair, *General's Life,* 464.

8. Murphy, Kondrashev, and Bailey, *Battleground Berlin,* 6–8; and Dujmovic, "Drastic Actions Short of War," 782.

9. Critchfield, *Partners at the Creation,* 25.

10. John Lewis Gaddis, *The Cold War: A New History* (New York: Penguin Press, 2005), 8–9.

11. Murphy, Kondrashev, and Bailey, *Battleground Berlin,* 12.

12. Richelson, *Spying on the Bomb,* 27.

13. Ibid., 28.

14. Ibid., 56–62.

15. Murphy, Kondrashev, and Bailey, *Battleground Berlin,* 36.

16. Thomas Borghardt, "America's Secret Vanguard: US Army Intelligence Operations in Germany, 1944–47," *Studies in Intelligence* 57, no. 2 (June 2013): 14.

17. Critchfield, *Partners at the Creation*, 21, 25.

18. Ibid., 32–33.

19. Borghardt, "America's Secret Vanguard," 2.

20. Critchfield, *Partners at the Creation*, 34.

21. Murphy, Kondrashev, and Bailey, *Battleground Berlin*, 15–17.

22. Ibid., 25.

23. Borghardt, "America's Secret Vanguard," 10.

24. Donald P. Steury, ed., *On the Front Lines of the Cold War: Documents on the Intelligence War in Berlin, 1946 to 1961* (Washington, DC: Central Intelligence Agency, Center for the Study of Intelligence, 1999), 10–13.

25. Critchfield, *Partners at the Creation*, 42–43, 45–47, 83.

26. Murphy, Kondrashev, and Bailey, *Battleground Berlin*, 55; and Steury, *Front Lines of the Cold War*, 140–45.

27. Bradley and Blair, *General's Life*, 467.

28. Murphy, Kondrashev, and Bailey, *Battleground Berlin*, 55.

29. Ibid., 56.

30. Bradley and Blair, *General's Life*, 474.

31. George F. Kennan, *Memoirs: 1925–1950* (Boston: Little, Brown, 1967), 421.

32. Murphy, Kondrashev, and Bailey, *Battleground Berlin*, 69.

33. Bradley and Blair, *General's Life*, 477–81.

34. Murphy, Kondrashev, and Bailey, *Battleground Berlin*, 62–75.

35. Critchfield, *Partners at the Creation*, 86–87.

36. Ibid., 122, 200. "Es wird ein Nachrichtendienst gegrundet," February 20, 1956. The FRG was founded in September 1949.

37. Critchfield, *Partners at the Creation*, 123.

38. Ibid., 62–65.

39. James V. Milano and Patrick Brogan, *Soldiers, Spies, and the Rat Line: America's Undeclared War against the Soviets* (Washington, DC: Brassey's, 1995), 4–5, 43–47.

40. Ibid., 73–74.

41. L. Britt Snider, *The Agency and the Hill: CIA's Relationship with Congress, 1946–2004* (Washington, DC: Central Intelligence Agency, Center for the Study of Intelligence, 2008), 141.

42. Ibid., 8–10.

43. Barrett, *CIA and Congress*, 31.

44. Ibid., 120; Snider, *Agency and the Hill*, 162; and Hayden B. Peake, "Harry S. Truman on CIA Covert Operations," *Studies in Intelligence* (Spring 1981): 35.

45. Bradley and Blair, *General's Life*, 487.

46. Ibid., 501–2.

47. Ibid., 507–11.

48. Clifford with Holbrooke, *Counsel to the President*, 130.

49. Hugh Wilford, *The Mighty Wurlitzer: How the CIA Played America* (Cambridge: Harvard University Press, 2008), 22.

50. Barrett, *CIA and Congress*, 25.

51. Clifford with Holbrooke, *Counsel to the President*, 168; and Wilford, *Mighty Wurlitzer*, 24.

52. Dujmovic, "Drastic Actions Short of War," 784.

53. Wilford, *Mighty Wurlitzer*, 25.

54. Snider, *Agency and the Hill*, 161; and Barrett, *CIA and Congress*, 32.

55. Evan Thomas, *The Very Best Men: Four Who Dared: The Early Years of the CIA* (New York: Simon and Schuster, 1995), 29; and Dujmovic, "Drastic Actions Short of War," 786–87.

56. Thomas, *Very Best Men*, 22.

57. Ibid., 23.

58. Ibid., 24.

59. Wilford, *Mighty Wurlitzer*, 25–27.

60. Dujmovic, "Drastic Actions Short of War," 786–87.

61. Thomas, *Very Best Men*, 87.

62. Ibid., 35.

63. Lowe, *Savage Continent*.

64. Thomas, *Very Best Men*, 36–39.

65. Ibid., 42, quoting Peter Sichel.

66. Steury, *Front Lines of the Cold War*, 111–12.

67. Ibid.

68. "Remembering CIA's Heroes: Douglas S. Mackiernan," last updated April 30, 2013, Central Intelligence Agency, https://www.cia.gov/news-information/featured-story-archive/2010-featured-story-archive/douglas-s.-mackiernan.html.

69. Thomas, *Very Best Men*, 51–52.

70. Wilford, *Mighty Wurlitzer*, 7.

71. Snider, *Agency and the Hill*, 40.

72. Peake, "Harry S. Truman on CIA," 35; Barrett, *CIA and Congress*, 120; and Snider, *Agency and the Hill*, 162.

73. Snider, *Agency and the Hill*, 260.

74. Clifford with Holbrooke, *Counsel to the President*, 165.

75. Walter Trohan interview, October 7, 1970, Harry S. Truman Presidential Library, http://www.trumanlibrary.org/oralhist/trohan.htm.

76. William J. Bray interview, August 1964, Harry S. Truman Presidential Library, http://www.trumanlibrary.org/oralhist/brayw.htm; and Harry S. Truman, *Mr. Citizen* (New York: Bernard Geis Associates, 1960), 147.

77. Paul Stillwell, *Battleship Missouri: An Illustrated History* (Annapolis, MD: Naval Institute Press, 1996), 95–96.

78. George S. Leonard to DCI RHH, 1 May 1947, Central Intelligence Agency, CADRE, C02135304; RHH to Leonard, 13 May 1947, Central Intelligence Agency, CADRE, C02135304; and Souers to RHH, 16 May 1947, Central Intelligence Agency, CADRE, C02111505.

79. *Diary, Rear Admiral R. H. Hillenkoetter, Director of Central Intelligence, May-September 1947*, CIA-RDP80R01731R002600430001-0, approved for release November 4, 2003, NARA, NACP.

80. McCullough, *Truman*, 419.

81. Walter Isaacson and Evan Thomas, *The Wise Men: Six Friends and the World They Made* (New York: Simon and Schuster, 1986), 446.

82. Darling, "DCI Hillenkoetter," 54–55.

83. Thomas, *Very Best Men*, 73–74.

84. Barrett, *CIA and Congress*, 49.

85. Snider, *Agency and the Hill*, 193.

86. Ibid.; and Barrett, *CIA and Congress*, 63.

87. Jack Davis, "The Bogotazo: Distant Events Shape the Craft of Intelligence," *Studies in Intelligence* (Fall 1967).

88. Barrett, *CIA and Congress*, 35.

89. Ibid., 37; and Snider, *Agency and the Hill*, 194.

90. Richelson, *Spying on the Bomb*, 67.

91. Bradley and Blair, *General's Life*, 517; and Benson and Warner, *Venona*.

92. Richelson, *Spying on the Bomb*, 76.

93. Ibid., 75.

94. Ibid., 81.

95. Ibid., 84.

96. Barrett, *CIA and Congress*, 57, 63; and Andrew, *For the President's Eyes Only*, 177.

97. Richelson, *Spying on the Bomb*, 90–91.

98. Ibid., 93.

99. Andrew and Mitrokhin, *Sword and the Shield*.

100. Barrett, *CIA and Congress*, 66.

101. Burton Hersh, *The Old Boys: The American Elite and the Origins of the CIA* (New York: Charles Scribner's Sons, 1992), 442–43.

102. Barrett, *CIA and Congress*, 71–81.

103. DCI Roscoe H. Hillenkoetter to Carmel Offie, May 17, 1950, Central Intelligence Agency, CADRE, C02128937.

104. Truman, *Years of Trial and Hope*, 331.

105. Murphy, Kondrashev, and Bailey, *Battleground Berlin*, 79, 85.

106. Ibid., 88.

107. Barrett, *CIA and Congress*, 84–89.

108. Snider, *Agency and the Hill*, 195; and Barrett, *CIA and Congress*, 84–89.

109. Dean Acheson interview, June 30, 1971, Harry S. Truman Presidential Library, http://www.trumanlibrary.org/oralhist/acheson.htm.

110. Kennan, *Memoirs*, 405.

111. Henhoeffer and Hanrahan, "Souers Speaks Out."

112. Allen W. Dulles, William H. Jackson, and Mathias F. Correa, *The Central Intelligence Agency and National Organization for Intelligence: A Report to the National Security Council,* Central Intelligence Agency, January 1, 1949, MORI ID: 401264:401264, 16.

113. Ibid., 18.

114. Ibid., 107.

115. Ibid., 135.

116. Ibid., 11.

117. Andrew, *For the President's Eyes Only,* 173–74.

118. Ludwell Lee Montague, *General Walter Bedell Smith as Director of Central Intelligence, October 1950–February 1953* (University Park: Pennsylvania State University Press, 1992), 36, 53.

119. Department of State, *Foreign Relations of the United States (FRUS), 1945–1950, Emergence of the Intelligence Establishment,* document 398, September 8, 1949 (Washington, DC, 1996), 1011.

120. Jeffrey T. Richelson, *The Wizards of Langley: Inside the CIA's Directorate of Science and Technology* (Boulder, CO: Westview Press, 2001), 16.

121. Donald P. Steury, *Sherman Kent and the Board of National Estimates: Collected Essays* (Washington, DC: Central Intelligence Agency, Center for the Study of Intelligence, 1994), xix.

122. Montague, *General Walter Bedell Smith,* 36, 55–56.

123. Henhoeffer and Hanrahan, "Souers Speaks Out."

124. John McCormack, "Tribute to Rear Adm. Roscoe H. Hillenkoetter, Director of Central Intelligence," *Congressional Record,* August 22, 1950.

125. President Harry S. Truman to Roscoe H. Hillenkoetter, 10 October 1950, Harry S. Truman Presidential Library.

126. Hillenkoetter to Truman, October 6, 1950, Harry S. Truman Presidential Library.

127. Andrew, *For the President's Eyes Only,* 170.

128. Bradley and Blair, *General's Life,* 552–53.

129. Barrett, *CIA and Congress,* 91.

130. "National Affairs: Soldier for Sailor," *Time,* August 28, 1950.

131. Snider, *Agency and the Hill,* 43.

132. Montague, *General Walter Bedell Smith,* 57.

133. Henhoeffer and Hanrahan, "Souers Speaks Out."

134. Andrew, *For the President's Eyes Only,* 192–93.

135. Henhoeffer and Hanrahan, "Souers Speaks Out."

136. Andrew, *For the President's Eyes Only,* 161–62.

137. Stillwell, *Battleship Missouri,* 182; and Edward J. Marolda, "The Hungnam and Chinnampo Evacuations," in *Encyclopedia of the Korean War: Political, Social, and Military History,* ed. Spencer C. Tucker, (Santa Barbara: ABC-CLIO, 2000), https://

www.history.navy.mil/research/library/online-reading-room/title-list-alphabetically
/h/the-hungnam-and-chinnampo-evacuations.html.

138. "Admiral in New Career after 41 Years," *New York Times*, May 8, 1957; and
"Hillenkoetter Is Elected Banner Line's Director," *New York Times*, August 4, 1958.

139. "Air Force Order on 'Saucers' Cited: Pamphlet by the Inspector General
Called Objects a 'Serious Business,'" *New York Times*, February 28, 1960.

140. Gerald Haines, "The CIA's Role in the Study of UFOs, 1947–1990: A Die-
Hard Issue," *Studies in Intelligence* 39, no. 4 (1995): 83.

141. Peter Kihss, "Adm. Roscoe H. Hillenkoetter, 85, First Director of CIA, Dies,"
New York Times, June 21, 1982.

142. Troy, "Truman on CIA."

143. Peake, "Harry S. Truman on CIA," 31.

144. Ibid., 36–37.

145. McCullough, *Truman*, 479.

146. Andrew, *For the President's Eyes Only*, 171; Peake, "Harry S. Truman on CIA,"
37; and Dulles Memo, Harry S. Truman Presidential Library.

147. Barrett, *CIA and Congress*, 71–81.

148. Sale, "Admiral Sidney W. Souers and President Truman," 67; and Souers papers, Box 1, Harry S. Truman Presidential Library.

149. Sale, "Admiral Sidney W. Souers and President Truman," 71.

150. DCI Richard Helms to Mrs. Sidney W. Souers, 16 January 1973.

151. "Harry S. Truman, 1945–53," last updated July 7, 2008, Central Intelligence Agency, https://www.cia.gov/library/center-for-the-study-of-intelligence/csi
-publications/books-and-monographs/our-first-line-of-defense-presidential-
reflections-on-us-intelligence/truman.html.

Bibliography

Achenbach, Joel. "70 Years Later, a Test in New Mexico Casts a Shadow." *Washington Post*, July 16, 2015.

Adams, Henry H. *Witness to Power: The Life of Fleet Admiral William D. Leahy.* Annapolis, MD: Naval Institute Press, 1985.

Alvarez, David, and Eduard Mark. *Spying through a Glass Darkly: American Espionage against the Soviet Union, 1945–1946.* Lawrence: University Press of Kansas, 2016.

Andrew, Christopher. *For the President's Eyes Only: Secret Intelligence and the American Presidency from Washington to Bush.* New York: Harper Perennial, 1996.

Andrew, Christopher, and Vasili Mitrokhin. *The Sword and the Shield: The Mitrokhin Archive and the Secret History of the KGB.* New York: Basic Books, 1999.

Barrett, David M. *The CIA and Congress: The Untold Story from Truman to Kennedy.* Lawrence: University Press of Kansas, 2005.

Benson, Robert Louis, and Michael Warner, eds. *Venona: Soviet Espionage and the American Response, 1939–1957.* Washington, DC: National Security Agency and Central Intelligence Agency, 1996.

Boothe, Clare. "Europe in the Spring: An American Playwright Reports on a Continent's Last Days of Freedom." *Life*, July 29, 1940.

Borghardt, Thomas. "America's Secret Vanguard: US Army Intelligence Operations in Germany, 1944–47." *Studies in Intelligence* 57, no. 2 (June 2013).

Bradley, Omar N. and Clay Blair. *A General's Life: An Autobiography by General of the Army Omar N. Bradley.* New York: Simon and Shuster, 1983.

Brandt, Raymond P. "St. Louis Admiral Expected to Head U.S. Intelligence: May Get New Job." *St. Louis Post-Dispatch*, February 27, 1947.

Breneman, Gary M. "Lawrence R. Houston: A Biography." *Studies in Intelligence* 30, no. 1 (Spring 1986).

Brown, Anthony Cave. *The Last Hero: Wild Bill Donovan.* New York: Times Books, 1982.

Brownell, Will, and Richard N. Billings. *So Close to Greatness: A Biography of William C. Bullitt.* New York: Macmillan, 1987.

Bullitt, Orville H., ed. *For the President: Personal and Secret; Correspondence Between Franklin D. Roosevelt and William C. Bullitt.* Boston: Houghton Mifflin, 1972.

Casey, William. *The Secret War against Hitler.* Washington, DC: Regnery Gateway, 1988.

Central Intelligence Agency. "Remembering CIA's Heroes: Douglas S. Mackiernan." Last updated April 30, 3013. https://www.cia.gov/news-information/featured -story-archive/2010-featured-story-archive/douglas-s.-mackiernan.html.

Clifford, Clark, with Richard Holbrooke. *Counsel to the President: A Memoir.* New York: Random House, 1991.

Critchfield, James H. *Partners at the Creation: The Men Behind Postwar Germany's Defense and Intelligence Establishments.* Annapolis, MD: Naval Institute Press, 2003.

Darling, Arthur B. "The Birth of Central Intelligence." *Studies in Intelligence* 10, no. 2 (Spring 1966).

———. "Central Intelligence under Souers." *Studies in Intelligence* 12, no. 1 (Fall 1968).

———. "DCI Hillenkoetter: Soft Sell and Stick." *Studies in Intelligence* 13, no. 1 (Winter 1969).

———. "With Vandenberg as DCI Part 1: Some Functions Centralized." *Studies in Intelligence* 12, no. 3 (Summer 1968).

———. "With Vandenberg as DCI Part II: Coordination in Practice." *Studies in Intelligence* 12, no. 4 (Fall 1968).

Davis, Jack. "The Bogotazo: Distant Events Shape the Craft of Intelligence." *Studies in Intelligence* (Fall 1967).

Department of State. *Foreign Relations of the United States, 1945–1950: Emergence of the Intelligence Establishment.* Washington, DC, 1996.

Devenny, Patrick. "Captain John A. Gade, U.S. Navy: An Early Advocate of Central Intelligence." *Studies in Intelligence* 56, no. 3 (September 2012).

Dictionary of American Naval Fighting Ships: Dixie, Maryland, West Virginia (Washington, DC, Department of the Navy; Naval Historical Center).

Donovan, Robert J. *Conflict and Crisis: The Presidency of Harry S. Truman 1945– 1948.* Columbia: University of Missouri Press, 1977.

Dorwart, Jeffry M. *Conflict of Duty: The U.S. Navy's Intelligence Dilemma, 1919– 1945.* Annapolis, MD: Naval Institute Press, 1983.

Dujmovic, Nicholas. "Drastic Actions Short of War: The Origins and Applications of CIA's Covert Paramilitary Function in the Early Cold War." *Journal of Military History* 76, no. 3 (July 2012): 775–808.

Dulles, Allen W., William H. Jackson, and Mathias F. Correa. *The Central Intelligence Agency and National Organization for Intelligence: A Report to the National Security Council.* Washington, DC: Central Intelligence Agency, 1949.

Gaddis, John Lewis. *The Cold War: A New History.* New York: Penguin Press, 2005.

Gade, John A. *All My Born Days: Experiences of a Naval Intelligence Officer in Europe.* New York: Charles Scribner's Sons, 1942.

Glass, Charles. *Americans in Paris: Life and Death under Nazi Occupation.* New York: Penguin Press, 2010.

Goulden, Joseph C. *The Best Years: 1945–50.* New York: Atheneum, 1976.

Gould's St. Louis Directory for 1917. St. Louis: Gould Directory Co., 1917. http://dl.mo space.umsystem.edu/umsl/islandora/object/umsl%3A166303#page/1013/ mode/1up.

Grose, Peter. *Gentleman Spy: The Life of Allen Dulles.* London: Andre Deutsch, 1995.

Haines, Gerald. "The CIA's Role in the Study of UFOs, 1947–1990: A Die-Hard Issue." *Studies in Intelligence* 39, no. 4 (1995).

Harris, Mark Edward. "A Family's Brush with Infamy." *Los Angeles Times Magazine,* May 13, 2001.

Henhoeffer, William, and James Hanrahan. "Souers Speaks Out: Notes on the Early DCIs." *Studies in Intelligence* 33, no. 1 (Spring 1989).

Hersh, Burton. *The Old Boys: The American Elite and the Origins of the CIA.* New York: Charles Scribner's Sons, 1992.

Holmes, W. J. *Double-Edged Secrets: U.S. Naval Intelligence Operations in the Pacific during World War II.* Annapolis, MD: Naval Institute Press, 1979.

Hone, Thomas C., and Joseph R. Beckenbach Jr. *The Destruction of the Battle Line at Pearl Harbor.* US Naval Institute Proceedings, December 1977.

Isaacson, Walter, and Evan Thomas. *The Wise Men: Six Friends and the World They Made.* New York: Simon and Schuster, 1986.

Jansen, Danny D., and Rhodri Jeffries-Jones. "The Missouri Gang and the CIA." In *North American Spies: New Revisionist Essays*, edited by Rhodri Jeffries-Jones and Andrew Lownie, 144–66. Lawrence: University Press of Kansas, 1991.

Johnson, Thomas R. *American Cryptology during the Cold War, 1945–1989: Book 1: The Struggle for Centralization, 1945–1960.* National Security Agency, Center for Cryptologic History, 1995.

Juntunen, Kim M. "US Army Attaches and the Spanish Civil War, 1936–1939: The Gathering of Technical and Tactical Intelligence." Thesis, United States Military Academy, 1990.

Kahn, David. *The Codebreakers: The Story of Secret Writing.* New York: Macmillan, 1967.

Kennan, George F. *Memoirs: 1925–1950.* Boston: Little, Brown, 1967.

Kern, Gary. "How 'Uncle Joe' Bugged FDR." *Studies in Intelligence* 47, no. 1 (2003).

Kihss, Peter. "Adm. Roscoe H. Hillenkoetter, 85, First Director of CIA, Dies," *New York Times,* June 21, 1982.

Layton, Edwin T., Roger Pineau, and John Costello. *And I Was There: Pearl Harbor and Midway—Breaking the Secrets.* New York: William Morrow, 1985.

Leahy, Fleet Admiral William D. *I Was There: The Personal Story of the Chief of Staff to Presidents Roosevelt and Truman Based on His Notes and Diaries Made at the Time*. New York: McGraw-Hill, 1950.

Leviero, Anthony. "Coordinator of Security: Sidney Souers Brings Wide Training to the Task of Advising the President on National Defense." *New York Times Magazine*, April 24, 1949.

Lovell, Stanley P. *Of Spies and Stratagems*. Englewood Cliffs, NJ: Prentice Hall, 1963.

Lowe, Keith. *Savage Continent: Europe in the Aftermath of World War II*. New York: St. Martin's Press, 2012.

MacArthur II, Douglas. Oral interview, 1986–87. Library of Congress. www.loc.gov /item/mfdipbib000732.

MacEachin, Douglas J. *The Final Months of the War with Japan: Signals Intelligence, U.S. Invasion Planning, and the A-Bomb Decision*. Washington, DC: Central Intelligence Agency, Center for the Study of Intelligence, 1998.

Marolda, Edward J. "The Hungnam and Chinnampo Evacuations." In *Encyclopedia of the Korean War: Political, Social, and Military History*, edited by Spencer C. Tucker. Santa Barbara: ABC-CLIO, 2000. https://www.history.navy.mil /research/library/online-reading-room/title-list-alphabetically/h/the-hun-gnam-and-chinnampo-evacuations.html.

Masterman, J. C. *The Double-Cross System in the War of 1939 to 1945*. New Haven: Yale University Press, 1972.

McCullough, David. *Truman*. New York: Simon and Schuster, 1992.

McIntosh, Elizabeth P. *Sisterhood of Spies: The Women of the OSS*. New York: Dell, 1998.

Melton, H. Keith. *OSS Special Weapons and Equipment: Spy Devices of WW II*. New York: Sterling Publishing, 1992.

Milano, James V., and Patrick Brogan. *Soldiers, Spies, and the Rat Line: America's Undeclared War against the Soviets*. Washington, DC: Brassey's, 1995.

Miller, Merle. *Plain Speaking: An Oral Biography of Harry S. Truman*. New York: Berkley Publishing, 1974.

Montague, Ludwell Lee. *General Walter Bedell Smith as Director of Central Intelligence, October 1950–February 1953*. University Park: Pennsylvania State University Press, 1992.

Moore, Jeffrey M. *Spies for Nimitz: Joint Military Intelligence in the Pacific War*. Annapolis, MD: Naval Institute Press, 2004.

Murphy, David E., Sergei A. Kondrashev, and George Bailey. *Battleground Berlin: CIA vs KGB in the Cold War*. New Haven: Yale University Press, 1997.

Murphy, Robert Daniel. *Diplomat among Warriors*. New York: Doubleday, 1964.

Norris, John G. "A 'Maquis' Runs Our Central Intelligence: He's from the Missouri." *Washington Post*, May 4, 1947.

Office of the Chief of Naval Operations, Division of Naval Intelligence. *U-352 Sunk by U.S.C.G. Icarus 5-9-42: Post Mortems on Enemy Submarines, Serial no.*

2, O.N.I. 250 Series. Washington, DC: Government Printing Office, 1942. https://www.history.navy.mil/research/library/online-reading-room/title-list-alphabetically/u/u352-sunk-by-uscg-icarus.html.

Office of Naval Intelligence Records, Records Group 38, National Archives and Records Administration, Washington, DC.

Pace, Eric. "Douglas MacArthur 2nd, 88, Former Ambassador to Japan." *New York Times*, November 17, 1997.

Packard, Wyman H. *A Century of U.S. Naval Intelligence.* Washington, DC: Department of the Navy, 1996.

Peake, Hayden B. "Harry S. Truman on CIA Covert Operations." *Studies in Intelligence* (Spring 1981).

Persico, Joseph E. *Roosevelt's Secret War: FDR and World War II Espionage.* New York: Random House, 2001.

Rear Admiral Roscoe H. Hillenkoetter Biography, Washington, DC: US Navy Bureau of Personnel, May 27, 1947.

Rear Admiral Sidney W. Souers Biography. Washington, DC: Naval Historical Center, Biographies Branch 0I-023, 1952.

Richelson, Jeffrey T. *Spying on the Bomb: American Nuclear Intelligence from Nazi Germany to Iran and North Korea.* New York: W. W. Norton, 2006.

———. *The Wizards of Langley: Inside the CIA's Directorate of Science and Technology.* Boulder, CO: Westview Press, 2001.

Roosevelt, Kermit, ed. *War Report of the OSS (Office of Strategic Services).* 2 vols. New York: Walker and Co., 1976.

Rudgers, David F. *Creating the Secret State: The Origins of the Central Intelligence Agency, 1943–1947.* Lawrence: University of Kansas Press, 2000.

Sacquety, Troy J., ed. "Behind Enemy Lines in Burma: The Stuff of Intelligence Legend." *Studies in Intelligence*, no. 11 (Fall-Winter 2001).

Sale, Sara L. "Admiral Sidney W. Souers and President Truman." *Missouri Historical Review* 86 (October 1991): 55–71.

Schafers, Ted. "He Helped Make History: Rear Admiral Sidney W. Souers of St. Louis Played a Big Role in Shaping U.S. Policy Under Truman." *St. Louis Globe-Democrat,* October 9, 1966.

Schroeder, Richard E. "The Hitler Youth as a Paramilitary Organization." PhD diss., University of Chicago dissertation, 1975.

———. *Missouri at Sea: Warships with Show-Me State Names.* Columbia: University of Missouri Press, 2004.

Smith, Richard Harris. *OSS: The Secret History of America's First Central Intelligence Agency.* Guilford, CT: Lyons Press, 2005.

Snider, L. Britt. *The Agency and the Hill: CIA's Relationship with Congress, 1946–2004.* Washington, DC: Central Intelligence Agency, Center for the Study of Intelligence, 2008.

Spector, Ronald H. *Eagle against the Sun: The American War with Japan.* New York: Vintage Books, 1985.

Steury, Donald P., ed. *On the Front Lines of the Cold War: Documents on the Intelligence War in Berlin, 1946 to 1961.* Washington, DC: Central Intelligence Agency, Center for the Study of Intelligence, 1999.

———. *Sherman Kent and the Board of National Estimates: Collected Essays.* Washington, DC: Central Intelligence Agency, Center for the Study of Intelligence, 1994.

Stillwell, Paul. *Battleship Missouri: An Illustrated History.* Annapolis, MD: Naval Institute Press, 1996.

Thomas, Evan. *The Very Best Men: Four Who Dared: The Early Years of the CIA.* New York: Simon and Schuster, 1995.

Troy, Thomas F. *Donovan and the CIA: A History of the Establishment of the Central Intelligence Agency.* Frederick, MD: University Publications of America, 1981.

———. "Truman on CIA." *Studies in Intelligence* 20, no. 1 (Spring 1976): 21-38.

Truman, Harry S. *Mr. Citizen.* New York: Bernard Geis Associates, 1960.

———. *Years of Trial and Hope.* Vol. 2, *Memoirs by Harry S. Truman.* New York: Doubleday, 1956.

United States Naval Academy. *Lucky Bag 1920.* Annapolis, MD, 1920.

US Naval History and Heritage Command. "Doris Miller 12 October 1919–24 November 1943." Posted April 20, 2015. https://www.history.navy.mil/re search/histories/biographies-list/bios-m/miller-doris.html.

US Naval History and Heritage Command. "*USS West Virginia's* Action Report, 11 December 1941." Posted December 9, 2014. https://www.history.navy .mil/browse-by-topic/diversity/african-americans/miller/uss-west-virginias-ac tion-report.html.

Vice Admiral Roscoe H. Hillenkoetter. Washington, DC: Naval Historical Center, Biographies Branch 0I-450, 1957.

Warner, Michael. *The Office of Strategic Services: America's First Intelligence Agency.* Washington, DC: Central Intelligence Agency, 2002.

———. "Salvage and Liquidation: The Creation of the Central Intelligence Group." *Studies in Intelligence* 39 (1996).

Warner, Michael, ed. *CIA Cold War Records: The CIA under Harry Truman.* Washington, DC: Central Intelligence Agency, Center for the Study of Intelligence, 1994.

Weadon, Patrick D. *The Battle of Midway: AF Is Short of Water.* Fort Meade, MD: National Security Agency, Center for Cryptologic History, 2000. https://www .nsa.gov/about/cryptologic-heritage/historical-figures-publications/publications /wwii/battle-midway.shtml.

Wilford, Hugh. *The Mighty Wurlitzer: How the CIA Played America.* Cambridge: Harvard University Press, 2008.

Winks, Robin W. *Cloak and Gown, 1939–1961: Scholars in the Secret War.* New York: William Morrow, 1987.

Yardley, Herbert O. *The American Black Chamber.* New York: Ballantine Books, 1981.

Index